Farm Trouble

Farm Trouble

BY LAUREN SOTH

PRINCETON, NEW JERSEY

PRINCETON UNIVERSITY PRESS

1957

L.C. CARD 57-5459

LAUREN SOTH is editor of the editorial pages of the
Des Moines Register and Tribune. He has been an
associate professor of economics at Iowa State College
and editor of the *Agricultural Situation* in the United
States Department of Agriculture. He won a Pulitzer
prize in 1955 for his editorials suggesting and pro-
moting the exchange of agricultural delegations with
the Soviet Union. When the exchange materialized,
he toured the Soviet Union as a member of the
American delegation.

Printed in the United States of America
by Princeton University Press, Princeton, New Jersey

Preface

This book is a report on some of America's most difficult social and economic problems—those connected with the adjustment of agriculture to a growing industrial economy. It is also a proposal for change in public policies related to farming.

The United States has had nearly a quarter-century of experience with government farm programs designed to support farmers' incomes and to help adjust agricultural production to changing market demand. This book contends that we are not taking advantage of the lessons from this experience. Acreage controls have not been successful, yet we continue to employ them. Price supports limited to a few basic crops have not done a good job of stabilizing total farm income. The methods used to protect prices of farm products have seriously misdirected production and interfered with an agreed national policy of freeing the channels of foreign trade.

Moreover, our public efforts have been timid at best so far as the fundamental problems of farm adjustment are concerned. One-third of American farm families live in poverty even during boom times. Their farming techniques are archaic. They are outside the stream of twentieth century progress. This is more than a farm problem—it is a national social cancer which an enlightened democracy cannot tolerate. We need a "Point Four" program of technical assistance here at home, along with a vigorous effort to reemploy and relocate people not needed in agriculture.

Commercial farming is faced with the possibility of another long depression, a cost-price squeeze, like that of the 1920's. The basic cause is a powerful tendency for farm output to grow faster than the demand for farm products. In most industries a larger volume means a larger gross income. In agriculture a larger total supply often means *less* gross income. The American farmer's unexcelled productiveness has turned like a Frankenstein's monster to injure its creator.

To many people, city and farm dwellers alike, it seems ridiculous that the United States should be troubled with surpluses when two-thirds of the world's peoples are short of food. It *is* ridiculous, of course; it is crazy. This is a crazy world in lots of ways. It is not easy to give away food. Farmers in countries which are short of food do not want the United States to ship low-priced or free food in competition with their products. Farmers in other food-exporting countries, such as Australia and Argentina, resent American food gifts or cut-rate sales to countries which are their customers.

Nevertheless, the United States should be trying constantly to increase exports of farm products. It should never give up seeking new ways to make effective use of its bountiful food production. In some countries it may be possible to establish food-distribution programs, outside the normal channels of trade, which will not offend local producers or competitive exporters. Any action which would increase the dollar buying power of food-short countries would help solve the farm surplus problem. This means, primarily, larger imports into the United States. But not many industries suffering import competition want to make this kind of contribution to ending the farm surplus.

The tendency to surplus production in American agriculture will be with us for some time to come. Even if production controls worked smoothly and efficiently, which they do not as our experience shows, we should try to expand consumption both at home and abroad. It goes against the moral grain of most Americans to restrain food output so long as hunger exists in the world.

If the nation does *not* want to restrain food production while people are hungry, then the farmer should not have to bear the entire cost of this welfare program. Farmers cannot afford to produce abundantly when this means low incomes, lower than the average for nonfarm people. They would prefer to produce without restraint. But they will call on government to help them cut production and raise prices if that is the only way they can increase their incomes.

Many of our public policies tend to worsen the imbalance between farm product supply and demand and should therefore be changed. Instead of trying to plan agricultural production in detail by means of acreage controls; instead of trying to buttress farm income by price supports which encourage excessive output of certain crops—this book suggests that agricultural subsidies be paid in direct form. It suggests that subsidies for genuine soil conservation be increased to replace parity price-fixing crop loans and government purchases. It argues that open subsidies, not related to the prices of individual commodities, are more consistent with a private enterprise economy.

Contents

Farm Trouble

1
The Continuing Debate

A great controversy is raging over agricultural policy in the United States.

It will not be settled in the 1950's or the 1960's. It is a continuing great debate like the 150-year dispute over tariff policy, which was not settled by Henry Clay's victory for protectionism in the Tariff Act of 1824 or by Cordell Hull's victory for freer trade in the Reciprocal Trade Agreements Act of 1934.

City people may think it strange that agricultural policy figures so importantly in the American political scene today when farm people have dwindled in numbers to only about 13 per cent of the population and are still declining. But this is precisely the reason *why* farm policies are in the foreground of the political picture. Agriculture is a declining industry— an industry of low returns. Despite the rapid decrease in number of farms and number of workers, American agriculture still has a great adjustment to make. Despite much political agitation and much government effort in the last quarter-century, the nation has not been able to achieve a full response of agriculture to a prosperous and growing general economy and to agriculture's own technological revolution. Too many people still depend on farming for a living.

Except during wartime, much of American agriculture has been in financial difficulties since 1920. Farmers suffered a severe squeeze between the prices they receive and the costs they pay during the 1920's when the economy as a whole was booming. The same sort of squeeze has reappeared now in the 1950's and threatens to be with us for some time. After years of experimenting with government farm programs, no magic-wand solutions have appeared to resolve the farm paradox—the paradox of bountiful production and low income for the producers of the bounty.

Nor will "letting nature take its course" cure the patient. Some people apparently believe that the farm problem will disappear if you can make the visible evidence of it disappear—just liquidate the large surpluses of grain, cotton, and dairy products and turn farmers loose to make the best of it. Unfortunately, the ailment we are dealing with is more chronic than that. The forces of "natural" adjustment grind very slowly and painfully. The American people are unwilling to put farming through the wringer of a long drawn-out agricultural depression. That is why they generally have approved the many government programs to help farmers in the years since 1920.

In some quarters, to be sure, there is a tendency to write off the farmers' complaints as those of cry-babies. For example, here are some sentences from an editorial by Editor John Fischer in *Harper's* in December 1955:

"Our pampered tyrant, the American farmer, is about to get his boots licked again by both political parties.

"Before next November's elections, Democrats and Republicans alike will be groveling all over the barnyard as they court the country vote—but the Democratic antics will be the most embarrassing. Nearly all Democratic politicians are now convinced that the farmers offer the largest single block of detachable votes—and many seem willing to use almost any tool of demagoguery which promises to pry it loose from the Republican grasp. . . .

"The record of recent elections indicates that the farmer is generally eager to sell his vote to the highest bidder, and that city people are too indifferent (or benumbed) to resent this legalized corruption, even when the bribe is lifted right out of their own pockets. But don't blame the politicians for this record. They didn't make it. We did—all of us.

"Our only excuse is that for 20 years—from 1920 until 1940—the farmers were in pretty bad shape. During these decades, city people got in the habit of giving them handouts, and haven't yet discovered that times have changed.

"The farmer not only got in the habit of accepting his dole; he came to believe that it belonged to him permanently, as a matter of right. When any hog keeps his jowls in the trough long enough, he gets to thinking he owns the trough."

Not much of this sort of thing gets printed or spoken publicly, but enough does to indicate that some city people view the farm problem as a simple issue of whether farmers get government handouts or not—as though no other economic group received any subsidies, open or disguised!

On the other hand, many farm leaders and politicians approach the problems of agriculture in an equally oversimplified way. They see the answer to all farm troubles in higher prices for farm products. Edward A. O'Neal, president of the American Farm Bureau Federation during the 1930's and 40's, used to tell of a conversation between Samuel Gompers, the great labor leader, and himself. O'Neal said to Gompers, "Sam, you have had great success in organizing labor to work for its own interests. I am starting out to help farmers as you helped labor. Have you some advice for me?"

"I surely have," said Gompers. "The American Federation of Labor is interested in much more than wages for its members. But it does not stress these other things. We pick out one thing, simple, that everybody can understand, wages, and fight hard to raise them. You must do the same."

O'Neal then said, "I suppose then that you would say higher prices for the farmer is what the Farm Bureau should fight for."

"I surely would," replied Gompers.*

* John D. Black of Harvard University repeated this story in his presidential address to the American Economic Association in December 1955.

Under Ed O'Neal, the Farm Bureau did fight for higher prices for the farmer by means of government price supports. In more recent years, during the presidencies of Allan B. Kline and Charles Shuman, the Farm Bureau has stood for moderation in government price guarantees. The Farm Bureau opposed the Democratic administrations of Harry Truman on price support policy, and it backed the Eisenhower administration in its effort to reduce price supports. Though the Farm Bureau is by far the largest and strongest of the major farm organizations, its moderation has not prevailed. The "farm bloc" in congress in the postwar years usually has advocated and been able to maintain high price supports for agriculture—high in the sense that they have kept basic crop prices far above world levels.

The explanation may be partly that other farm organizations, especially the National Farmers Union, have exerted pressure for higher price guarantees, and partly that commodity groups within the Farm Bureau itself have done the same. Also, it may be that most congressmen believe Farm Bureau spokesmen do not truly reflect the opinion of the rank and file. Several congressmen have asserted this, and public opinion polls in some midwestern states indicate that there may be truth in it.

At any rate, the political appeal in the Gompers dictum of a "simple" drive for higher price guarantees for farmers has been a powerful one since the end of World War II. When the government promised farmers high prices for their products as an incentive to get more production during the war, it was generally understood that the guarantees would be lowered after the war, allowing a reasonable time for farmers to adjust. In 1948, Congress passed a law providing for a gradual lowering of price guarantees. But this law never was permitted to go into effect. Congress kept postponing year by year the adjustment to a new price level until 1954. Then the new Republican administration pushed through Congress a modified version of the 1948 act. Under this law the Department of Agriculture lowered price supports on basic crops slightly for the year 1955. But in 1956, a presidential election year, the drive for a return to wartime price guarantees was renewed. It was strong enough to get a bill through Congress. President Eisenhower vetoed the bill, but in vetoing it he promised to raise the price supports by administrative action considerably above previously announced levels. Then Congress passed another farm bill, which the president signed, maintaining the major provisions of the 1954 law on price guarantees. This law permits the administration to adjust price supports for certain designated "basic" commodities according to the supplies of those commodities. But the range is a narrow one, and the Eisenhower administration proved during the 1956 Congressional debate that it would respond to political pressures in setting the level of price supports.

The farm policy controversy since the end of World War II has centered largely on the level of price guarantees. It also has involved a number of other hot issues: how the government soil conservation programs should be conducted, and by which agency; whether the government should pay farmers direct subsidies in lieu of price supports; policy toward the small farmer as against the large; aid to the poorest farmers, especially in the South; tariffs and quotas on imports of farm products; the fight between butter and margarine; and many more. But prices have been the big issue.

The line-up of the contending forces on agricultural policy is difficult to describe, because the lines are mixed. In general the Republican party has taken the conservative side of farm questions: for lower price guarantees, for less interference by the government in farmers' decisions, for greater reliance on education and research to solve farm problems. In general the Democratic party has taken a more daring attitude toward government action. It has favored higher price guarantees, more aid to underprivileged farm families, and acreage and marketing controls. It has been willing to try direct subsidies instead of price support loans and purchases as a means of aiding the producers of perishable commodities.

Many Congressional Republicans, especially from the Midwest and Great Plains states, often side with the Democrats on price supports and other farm matters. And some Democrats—for example, Senator Clinton P. Anderson of New Mexico, who was secretary of agriculture under Harry Truman—line up with the Republicans on the same issues.

In Congress, farm policy tends to be fairly nonpartisan in comparison with policy on most other domestic issues. In the debate on the farm bill of 1954, Representative Walter Judd, Republican from Minnesota, said that the farmer was in trouble but not through his own fault or through the fault of Mr. Benson or Mr. Eisenhower, or Mr. Truman or Mr. Roosevelt. "The farm program, under which the farmers are having so much difficulty," said Judd, "was written by the farm bloc in congress. It did not pay any attention to Mr. Roosevelt, to Mr. Truman, to Mr. Brannan. It does not intend to pay any attention to what Mr. Eisenhower or Mr. Benson recommend."

There is much truth in this. In the last few years the farm bloc has not been nearly as solid, or voting on farm issues as nonpartisan, as in the twenties. In one key vote on the McNary-Haugen farm relief bill in 1927, 101 Republicans and 100 Democrats voted for it in the House; 68 Republicans and 53 Democrats voted against it. Obviously this was a non-party-line vote. In contrast, the vote on the key price support provision in the 1954 farm act was strongly along party lines. In the House, 182 Republicans and 45 Democrats voted for the administration bill; 147 Democrats and 23 Republicans voted against it. The same party breakdown showed up in the Senate vote. However, in 1956, Republican

Congressmen from farm districts were much less inclined to follow President Eisenhower than they were in 1954. This seems odd in view of the fact that 1956 was a presidential election year and Mr. Eisenhower's popularity was undiminished. But the difference between 1954 and 1956 was the sharp decline in farm income between the two years. Farmers, though not "in revolt" as some reports indicated, were unhappy about economic conditions in 1956 and were expressing themselves on policy matters more vociferously than before.

Agriculture Secretary Ezra Taft Benson had led many farmers to believe that he was fundamentally opposed to any government action to protect farm income. His speeches carried a tone of stern disapproval of government intervention in the farm business. And though Mr. Benson stated repeatedly that he favored price supports (at a modest level), conservation payments, and other aids to agriculture, he conveyed the impression that he disliked the whole set-up and would abandon it if he could. Moreover, Benson failed to use powers available to him to protect farmers against the very severe drop in hog prices in the last half of 1955—though farm organization leaders and midwestern Republican politicians urged him to act.

Mr. Benson, True Morse, his undersecretary of agriculture, and Earl Butz, one of the assistant secretaries, all are stanch conservatives. Their speeches appeal to many farmers during good times. But at a time when farm income is on the skids, few farmers like to be told they should take it on the chin and not call on the government. This was the way many pronouncements from the Department of Agriculture sounded to farmers in 1954-55.

Thus in 1956, Republican congressmen were reflecting a considerable amount of farmer dissatisfaction with the Benson administration of the Department of Agriculture and with the "flexible" price supports which Benson advocated.

CHART 1. National and Farm Income

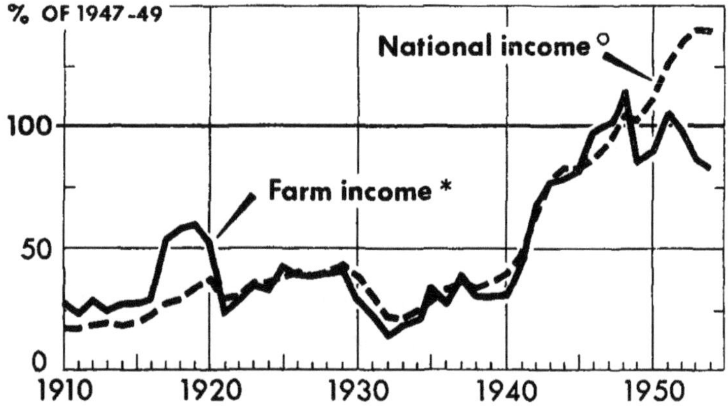

% OF 1947-49

National income °

Farm income *

100

50

0

1910   1920   1930   1940   1950

* FARM INCOME REFERS TO NET INCOME FROM AGRICULTURAL SOURCES TO PERSONS LIVING ON FARMS
° DEPARTMENT OF COMMERCE ESTIMATES OF NATIONAL INCOME HAVE BEEN ADJUSTED TO MAKE THEM
  COMPARABLE WITH FARM INCOME ESTIMATES

U. S. DEPARTMENT OF AGRICULTURE   NEG. 1729-55(11) AGRICULTURAL MARKETING SERVICE

The party regularity on farm policy did not hold up as well as in 1954.

The election year 1956 was the fifth year of a steady decline in farm income following the Korean war peak. It brought out any latent tendencies of politicians to jump over party lines on the farm issue and greatly emphasized the "farm vote" in politicians' minds. It also brought about some changes in party positions. The Republican administration retreated from some of the policies which had been strongly emphasized in the 1952 presidential campaign and in the 1954 Congressional campaign.

As late as the summer of 1955, Secretary Benson and Undersecretary Morse had said they were opposed to direct subsidies to farmers for leaving crop acreage idle. The farm organizations, even including the Farm Bureau, advocated a "soil bank" plan—under which farmers would be paid to reduce acreages of basic crops below the regular allotments

CHART 2. Farm and Nonfarm Income per Person

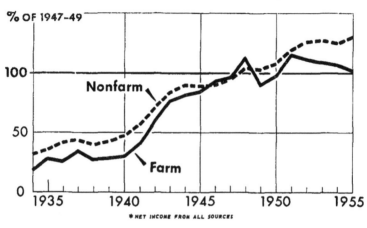

% OF 1947-49

100

50

0

Nonfarm

Farm

1935   1940   1945   1950   1955

* NET INCOME FROM ALL SOURCES

U. S. DEPARTMENT OF AGRICULTURE   NEG. 1797-56 (10)   AGRICULTURAL MARKETING SERVICE

of the established program. Mr. Benson would have none of it. But by January of 1956 he was persuaded that the soil bank was a good idea. President Eisenhower presented such a plan to Congress in a special farm message, and the administration forces in Congress carried it through to enactment.

The administration also responded to the demand for higher price supports for 1956 crops, as has been mentioned earlier.

After the 1956 farm act was passed, the question arose as to whether the soil bank feature could become effective that year. At first, Secretary Benson said it could not, because many crops had already been planted by May, when the law was passed. A few days later he said his department would try to get it in operation. But he said he would not be in favor of letting farmers plow up acreage already planted. The Republican party for more than twenty years had been denouncing the Democrats, especially Henry A. Wallace, the New Deal secretary of agriculture, for plowing up cotton in the early thirties. By June, however, Mr. Benson had given in on this too. He announced that farmers could plow up or clip oats or corn and place this land in the soil bank so as to receive payments.

The rigid principles of "free enterprise," moderate price supports (as a protection only against "disaster," as Secretary Benson said soon after taking office), limited crop controls, if any, and no direct subsidies had been virtually abandoned by the Republicans.

Congressmen running for election in 1956 went even further than the administration. Senator Bourke Hickenlooper of Iowa, a regular Republican who had supported the administration all the way on agricultural policy, proposed a radical new method of emergency farm aid in the winter of 1955-56. Hog prices had sunk to about $11 a hundred pounds in December 1955. Hickenlooper proposed that farmers be given a subsidy payment for selling sows and gilts, in order to cut the production of pigs in 1956. This was reminiscent of the sow and pig slaughter program of Henry Wallace in 1933, which was so fiercely condemned by the Republicans. However, Mr. Benson did not like the idea, and Hickenlooper did not push it.

Many congressmen who had favored "flexible" (lower) price supports switched over to the "rigid" (higher) support side of the debate in 1956. Republican governors in the Middle West met to discuss farm problems and put the heat on Secretary Benson to use his authority to buy pork to bolster the price of hogs. Benson did inaugurate a modest pork-buying program, but it was not enough of a program to have an appreciable effect on prices.

One big reason for all this furor about farm affairs among the candidates for office may have been the memory of the presidential election of 1948. In that election Harry Truman surprised the opinion pollsters and the politicians by defeating Governor Thomas Dewey—largely, it was believed, because of his swinging of the farmers' votes in the Middle West. The circumstances were persuasive: Truman unquestionably turned the tide in his direction during the late weeks of the campaign, and he was attacking the Republican Congress bitterly on farm issues during those weeks. This interpretation of the 1948 Truman victory has been convincingly challenged; to say the least, it is over-simplified. But regardless of that, the important thing is many politicians believed it.

The 1948 election undoubtedly has had profound effects on farm policy since then. Until that time, the major farm organizations, the Department of Agriculture, and both political parties were agreed on the principle of a so-called "sliding scale" of price supports to replace the "fixed" guarantees of the war and preceding postwar years. After 1948 most Democrats, the Farmers Union, and the "farm bloc" in Congress abandoned the sliding scale idea. Mr. Truman and his secretary of agriculture, Charles F. Brannan, had plugged hard for "high, rigid" price supports in the campaign.

Another landmark in the postwar history of farm policy was the sweeping proposal for change made by Secretary Brannan in 1949. Brannan suggested a much more inclusive system of price supports. Instead of guaranteeing farmers minimum prices only for the legally designated "basic" crops —cotton, rice, peanuts, tobacco, corn, and wheat—Brannan would have included virtually all farm products. Many "nonbasic" products had been included under the wartime guarantees but were dropped soon after the war. Brannan also proposed a higher price support level, based on maintaining a certain share of the national income for farmers. And he advocated direct payments to farmers in lieu of price support for perishable commodities. That is, farmers would be paid the difference in cash between the market price and the government-guaranteed price.

This proposal stirred up the most violent controversy over farm policy since the early days of the New Deal. Farm Bureau President Allan Kline, a dedicated believer in individual economic freedom and free markets, tore into the fray as the leader of the anti-Brannanites. Republicans generally, other Farm Bureau leaders, the National Grange, and nearly all other farm groups except the Farmers Union sided with Kline. The quarrel became bitterly personal at times.

At the National Farm Institute, sponsored by the Chamber of Commerce in Des Moines in 1950, Brannan and Kline met on the platform in a panel-discussion session. Though four other participants were on the panel, it turned into a Brannan-Kline debate.

Both men lost their tempers. Kline spoke first and said that in his opinion no real discussion with Secretary Brannan would be possible, because the secretary was "frankly and aggressively partisan and political." Brannan said he admitted he was political and that he had campaigned for the election of Harry Truman. Then he took a crack at Kline: "There still appears to be some misconception and lack of understanding about these farm program recommendations, and even my motives for making them. Some of this is a natural result of insufficient information. In all candor and without malice, I say that more of it has been intentionally manufactured by the leadership of a great farm organization."

"Boo!" came from many in the audience, which included a large number of Iowa Farm Bureau members and friends of Allan Kline, a Vinton, Iowa, farmer who had advanced to the national presidency of the Bureau.

"Thank you, gentlemen . . . ," said Brannan, a little flustered.

"Boo!" came from the audience again, followed by a round of loud applause.

Later, Secretary Brannan said, "I should like to ask the president of the American Farm Bureau Federation in all seriousness: does it aid agriculture in any way to say of the administration's proposals: 'People who propose such a program to farmers are very dumb or downright dishonest'?"

Kline denied that he had ever said the secretary of agriculture was dumb or dishonest. But he said he thought the problem of the underprivileged and underemployed in agriculture was not a price problem that could be solved by higher price supports. He said he did "ridicule the idea" of providing maybe another $140 a year to a farm family that has a gross income of only $700 in the first place. He said, "Anyone who presents such a problem as a price problem is either very dumb or dishonest." The important thing, he said, was to improve the productivity of the low-income farmer.

This debate undoubtedly intensified the personal antagonism between Brannan and Kline, and the Farm Bureau continued to wage unrelenting warfare against the Brannan Plan in total. Secretary Brannan cancelled a second debate with Kline which had been scheduled for the Minnesota Farm Forum in Minneapolis a week later. Because of the row between Brannan and Kline, relations between the Department of Agriculture and the Farm Bureau were at low ebb during the ensuing two years. Congress refused to pay serious attention to the agriculture secretary's proposals, and the general national political debate over agricultural policy degenerated into charges of "socialism" and "regimentation" on the one hand and charges of "selling the farmer down the river" and "favoritism to the big farmer" on the other hand.

This was unfortunate, because, with all its faults, the Brannan Plan did bring forward some new ideas for public discussion. And new ideas certainly have been needed. Under the postwar price support programs, the government had accumulated large quantities of eggs and potatoes which deteriorated in storage and had to be destroyed or used for livestock feed or fertilizer. Brannan proposed a way to avoid such waste. He said price supports for perishable products should be replaced by a system of direct payments to farmers of the difference between the market price and the support level. This was not really a new idea. It had been incorporated in the farm act passed by Congress in 1948. But this provision of the law had been changed in 1949, leaving the authority for direct payments uncertain. Secretary Brannan wanted to get a clear expression from Congress (and the money) to make direct payments possible.

Subsidies of a similar nature had been used during World War II to permit livestock producers to get higher returns than otherwise would have been possible under the price ceilings on meat.

After the war the American Farm Economic Association held a contest for papers on a new agricultural policy. The winning paper, written by Dr. William H. Nichols, now professor of agricultural economics at Vanderbilt University, suggested the direct payment plan. A large number of agricultural economists agreed that a payment program would be more sensible than government buying as a means of supporting prices of perishable products. Then Senator George Aiken, Vermont Republican, incorporated the idea in the legislation which was passed in 1948. Allan Kline himself in those early years expressed mild approval of the idea, at least as worth trying out. And the Iowa Farm Bureau Federation passed resolutions in favor of trying the payment plan on hogs.

Yet when Secretary Brannan proposed direct payments in 1949 the American Farm Bureau Federation attacked the scheme sharply and has ever since. In the presidential campaign of 1952 General Eisenhower referred to the Brannan Plan as having "immoral implications." An unfortunate consequence of all this rancor over the Brannan Plan has been that the method of direct payments to agriculture has received little serious political consideration. Curiously enough, however, the Eisenhower administration did approve of direct payments to wool producers in lieu of price support in the Farm Act of 1954.

Allan Kline and Charles Brannan personalized the extremes of the agricultural debate during the 1945-55 period. Kline was an Iowa farmer and hog producer, an exceptionally successful one, before moving up through the ranks of the Farm Bureau to its presidency. He was president of the Iowa Farm Bureau for several terms before becoming national president in 1947. In the early 30's he took part in the county administration of the first agricultural adjustment program. In those years he did not stand out as an opponent of federal farm programs.

But after he became president of the American Farm Bureau, he quickly achieved prominence as a strong advocate of individualism and an opponent of government intervention in agriculture. Kline is a brilliant leader, deeply sincere in his beliefs and extremely effective as a speaker and debater. He resigned from the top post of the Farm Bureau in 1953.

Charles Brannan, on the other hand, is equally dedicated to the idea that agriculture must have a considerable degree of government management. He is a lawyer who got his start in agricultural affairs as an attorney for the United States Department of Agriculture. He also is an intelligent advocate, a good speaker, and a sharp debater. He believes government must plan agricultural production in considerable detail and maintain a high, administered price level for farmers. Since the Republican victory in 1952, Brannan has been an attorney and official for the National Farmers Union. He ran for the Democratic nomination for the United States Senate in Colorado in 1956 but was defeated.

Kline and Brannan are at the poles of the farm debate. In

between them, in all farm organizations and in both political parties, are a great many agricultural leaders who believe in some government action in agriculture, but not in as much as does Brannan and not in as little as does Kline.

Below the political froth generated by the Brannan-Kline encounters, there has been a great deal of serious, nonpartisan study of agricultural policy during the post-World War II years. In no field of domestic economic policy has the nation had the benefit of as much expert study and opinion as in agricultural policy.

Professional agricultural economists probably have been closer to practical affairs in their field than economists specializing in any other branch of economic activity. Working in the land grant colleges, the Department of Agriculture, and the farm organizations, they have been participants in policy formation since the beginning of the postwar farm troubles of the twenties.

Such men as John D. Black of Harvard University; E. G. Nourse, former chairman of the president's Council of Economic Advisers; J. S. Davis, member of the current Council; Howard Tolley, former Department of Agriculture official and now with the National Planning Association; Theodore W. Schultz of the University of Chicago; O. B. Jesness of the University of Minnesota; Murray Benedict of the University of California; Walter W. Wilcox of the Library of Congress Legislative Reference Service; O. V. Wells, Sherman Johnson, and Frederick Waugh of the Department of Agriculture; T. K. Cowden of Michigan State University; Louis Bean, formerly of the Department of Agriculture; D. A. Fitzgerald of the International Cooperation Administration —have been key men in the writing of "farm plans," in the advisory councils of Congress, the Department of Agriculture, and the farm organizations, and in the many studies of agricultural policy by independent agencies.

There has been no lack of these studies. Research foundations, planning groups, and committees were busy on "the farm problem" during the first decade after World War II.

On a scholarly or independent level, farm policy reports by committees of the Land Grant College Association, the Farm Foundation, the Conference on Economic Progress, the National Planning Association, the Committee for Economic Development, the Twentieth Century Fund, and the American Assembly are especially notable. On the official level the policy or program planning reports by the Department of Agriculture under both Clinton Anderson and Charles Brannan were valuable contributions. Some of the reports by the Agriculture Committees of Congress and by the Joint Committee on the Economic Report have been enlightening additions to the literature on farm policy. The same could be said for some of the reports of the Council of Economic Advisers. On the pressure group level, all the major farm organizations and even some labor and business groups have published studies and reports on farm policy of surprising depth, understanding, and impartiality.

Despite all the erudite studies of the problems of farm adjustment, despite the many proposals for change in federal farm programs, these programs remain essentially the same now as they were in 1945-46. For example, take the matter of price supports. The overwhelming majority of expert opinion among agricultural economists and independent research groups advises considerably lower price supports for cotton and wheat. Yet Congress has prevented any substantial lowering of these guarantees. The majority of the experts also would vote for more flexible price guarantees not tied to a historical formula such as parity. But Congress, which at one time seemed to agree with this opinion, has narrowed the range of administrative discretion on price supports in recent years.

One reason why Congress has ignored the experts is that price guarantees have become identified with "doing something" for the farmer. Many of the experts, in advocating flexible price supports, have proposed alternative methods of supporting farm income—usually some kind of outright subsidy—during periods of industrial recession, lagging exports, or excess supply. But the leading political pressure groups which argue for flexible supports have proposed no substitute method of protecting farm income. They just want price guarantees lowered. Thus "flexible" price supports have become symbolic of little government action to help farmers. And "rigid" or high price supports have become symbolic of generous aid to agriculture. Many politicians in 1956 felt they had to "come out" for high price supports, even though they may have favored some other method of farm aid.

This is the way the political process works. The symbols sometimes become more important than the substance. This occurs because the general public, farmers included, is not sufficiently well informed to sift out the real issues from the false.

Let us turn now to some of the shibboleths which affect American farm policy.

2
The Shibboleths

Like any field of politics, agricultural politics in the United States has its "Thou shalts" and "Thou shalt nots." Perhaps farm policy is more plagued by shibboleths than public policy in any other area. Looking over the farm policies adopted by the national government in recent years, one might easily conclude that catchwords, slogans, and clichés have had more to do with establishing these national policies than facts or logic.

Candidates for public office, administrators of public agencies, even businesses which depend heavily on farmers as buyers or sellers must obey the rules of the game in farm affairs—or else. Four of these standard rules are so important that they may be said to dominate the making of agricultural policy. These are: Thou shalt invariably promote The Family Farm. Thou shalt elevate The Rural Life above urban life. Thou shalt steadfastly uphold Parity for the Farmer. Thou shalt blame the Middleman for any economic difficulties which overtake farmers.

Once a politician or a farm leader (who also is a politician of course) has learned his catechism on these major points, he is equipped to hit the hustings. He need not bother with many facts; he only needs to whip up the emotions of his listeners by frequent references to the key words given above, and he has arrived as a full-fledged farm politician.

Farmers are not more gullible than other groups of the population. Like the rest of us, they enjoy hearing themselves pictured as noble citizens who are entitled by divine law to more than they are getting. Let it be said, also, that these clichés about farm policy have a solid element of truth in them—that is why they have persisted so long and are still so powerful in public policy. But they have been overworked, and they have led to serious mistakes in the directions taken by some national farm programs.

The Family Farm

Since colonial days—maybe since the days of the sturdy, independent yeoman of the English Middle Ages—Anglo-Saxon peoples have placed high social value on the family farm. In the early growth of democratic government the independent small landowner played an important part. He was free to speak his mind "without fear or favor" when employees of the new factories, mines, and other collective economic institutions were not. He was the solid foundation of free suffrage, free speech, freedom of religion, and the other essentials of free government.

It is no wonder that a society which places so much stress on individual liberty and independence should also idealize the one-family farm. Even in modern times there is validity to the equation of family farming and political democracy. But modern democracy cannot depend on the preservation of the family farm. In the United States only 13 per cent of the people now live on farms of all kinds, and this percentage is still dwindling rapidly. No matter how free and independent farmers may be, they cannot preserve democracy by themselves. The great mass of citizens nowadays are employees, and if their will to remain politically free does not continue, then all of us are lost—farmers too. In short, the problem of maintaining freedom is only in small measure a matter of preserving the family farm.

It happens that economic development in the United States has not seriously weakened the position of the family farm as the basic economic organization in agriculture. The family farm which got established naturally in colonial days, in the northern states at least, and which was officially encouraged by the Homestead Act and other public policies, continues as the bulwark of American agriculture. The family farmer has held his own in general farming areas but has given way somewhat to large-scale "corporate" farms in fruits, vegetables, wheat farming, and some other specialized branches of agriculture. Family farms have been growing larger with increasing mechanization, but this has not increased the amount of hired labor. The trend toward large-scale farms with many hired laborers certainly has not become dominant in America. Yet the bugbear of the decline of the family farm regularly rears its head in farm politics.

I have said that there appears to be no important threat to the family-type farm operation in the United States. But let us suppose there is a real threat—let us suppose the people who worry about this are right and I am wrong. The question then becomes: Would it be desirable to construct public policies to prevent a change to some other form of organization—large-scale cooperative farms, corporation farms, or something else?

This is a matter of value judgments, and my own preference would be to sacrifice some economic advantages in order to preserve the American farm system as primarily an individual owner-operator or renter-operator system. But this system can hardly be defended realistically as the bedrock of democracy any longer—and not simply because the farm population is such a small proportion of the total. There is no evidence to indicate that farm people are any more devoted to the basic liberties of our constitutional system than other groups. And some evidence hints farm people are less concerned about these liberties. Opinion polls during the McCarthy spasm of infringements on individual freedom indicated that farm people were *less* opposed to McCarthyism than other groups. Polls taken in Iowa, Minnesota, and Wisconsin during the early 1950's showed farm residents less willing to uphold the right of free speech, free press, and free religious observance for minority groups, such as Jehovah's Witnesses, than were city folks.

Besides, the family farmer's vaunted independence is not what it was in earlier days. The farmer today is as closely dependent on other elements of the economy as anyone else. He no longer can exist as a truly self-sufficient enterpriser but must call upon off-farm suppliers not only for his household needs (even food) but also for his production necessities. He cannot operate without gasoline, for example. So the concept of the self-reliant individual farmer who asks nothing from anyone else and lives by the sweat of his brow is somewhat distorted for modern life. The difference between the city man who works for wages and the farmer who is his own boss is not so great as it was.

In any case, the opportunity to be your own boss evidently is not as compelling with farm people as many upholders of the family farm believe. Thousands of them willingly leave the farm for city jobs every year for higher incomes.

The farm politicians who orate so passionately about the family farm and its decline really are making little contribution to building a sound agricultural policy. They are raising a bogey that does not exist, or at least is not important, and thus tend to divert attention from more critical matters.

Marxist critics of the American economic system long have talked about the "disappearance" of the family farm, or the "tendency to accumulation" of land as Marx himself put it, under capitalism. The Marxists are not interested in preserving the family farm, of course. They are interested in fanning dissent and creating dissatisfaction. But their misinterpretation of the effects of economic development in this country often is swallowed by sincere, antisocialist agricultural leaders.

Strangely enough, both the conservatives and the liberals among farm leaders make use of the emotional appeal of the family farm. Those who object to government price supports, acreage controls, and other federal farm programs frequently charge that these are steps toward socialized or collective farming. These interventions into the private farm economy will mean the end of the family farm, they say. I have heard some Farm Bureau leaders take this line. The reasoning behind this is not very clear. Some Farm Bureau leaders have referred to "socialized agriculture" in England and Sweden as a foreboding of what will happen in the United States "if we continue the route we are traveling." But there has been no tendency toward collective farms in England or Sweden. More to the point, federal farm programs in the United States have not resulted in a growth of collective farming. The opponents of government price supports, acreage regulations, etc., have plenty of ammunition for their side of the argument without resorting to the "threat to the family farm" alarmism.

The farm leaders who favor government pricing, production controls, and even stronger government action in behalf of agriculture also use the "threat to the family farm" on their side of the argument. They claim large corporate farms are absorbing the family farms. They advocate limits on the size of farms eligible for government benefits and government action to raise incomes of family farmers. Farmers Union leaders have been especially vocal about the family farm as an argument for high price supports.

Thus we have one group of farm leaders advocating "free enterprise" as a way of saving the family farm, while another group of leaders advocates more government programs as a way of saving the family farm. It may be difficult for the ordinary citizen to tell which of these points of view is correct, since few of the contesting parties bother to provide any facts or even define what they mean by family farm. But of one thing we can be sure: *both* these arguments for the preservation of family farming cannot be correct.

There are *elements* of truth in both the Farm Bureau

story and the Farmers Union story, and there are elements of untruth or distortion. This is a perfect set-up for the demagogic appeal to an emotional concept.

The Rural Life

The advantages of rural living over city life have long been a subject of impassioned oratory, prose, and poetry. Any politician talking to farm groups cannot fail to talk of the values of living close to the soil, the character-building virtues of watching things grow, the quietude, the solitude, the nearness to God, the splendor of Nature, etc., etc. I am not being cynical about these things, for they are all true— and no one places a higher value on rural life than I. What I want to call attention to here, however, is the employment of this idealization of rural life to the disadvantage of farm people—and all the rest of us.

For years politicians have been talking of the nonmoney values in rural living to rationalize lower incomes and lower material levels of living for farm families. Many people are willing to sacrifice some income in order to live in the country. But they are not willing to sacrifice much, judging by their choices when they have an opportunity for choice.

The steady migration of people from farm to city itself is adequate evidence that the joys of the bucolic life will not offset much difference in hard cash. Also, the continued drive of farm people to urbanize their way of life indicates that the attractions of the city have pulling power too.

Farm people do *not* include in their concept of the rural life such things as outside plumbing, oil lamps, inadequate telephone service, poor library service (or none at all), poor schools, poor roads, inadequate housing. But the unstated implication of much of the glorification of rural life is that people ought to be willing to accept these hardships in order to get the advantages of life in the open spaces.

Nostalgia about life on the farm should not disguise the

fact that material conveniences are important. Nothing irritates me more than to read an editorial in a large-city newspaper about the virtues of life in the country, the freedom farm people enjoy, and so on—concluded by a question, implied or explicit: Why should farmers always be complaining about their incomes and wanting government help? Well, farmers appreciate their independence and their closeness to nature, but they do not like to be considered second-class citizens when it comes to the material aspects of life. The fact that farmers have insisted on action by the government to enable them to live more like their city cousins is proof that they do not think life in the country is its own reward.

The clichés about the rural life are not confined to city people. Farm leaders and farm people themselves often are blinded by traditionalism to their own best interests. Farm people and their organizations in many states have hindered the movement toward reorganization of school districts into larger administrative units, the abandonment of the one-room school, and the introduction of modern equipment and better teachers. Farmers often say that the old one-room school was good enough for them so it is good enough for their children.

The elevation of rural life above city life leads to the feeling that farm people are somehow more moral and better fitted to make decisions for the whole community than city people. This is a big factor in the continuing unfair representation in state legislatures, most of which are still apportioned as they were back in horse and buggy days. Business groups lend themselves to this corruption of representative government by lining up with farm groups to prevent redistricting. They fear the increased power that would accrue to labor unions if city people were fairly represented. Farm legislators are more conservative than city legislators generally and tend to be suspicious of the "evils" of the big cities and of labor leaders. Regardless of the moral attributes of the rural life, this is a contradiction of the representative form of government to which farmers, like everybody else, declare allegiance.

Glorification of farm life has been a hindrance in developing national policies which would facilitate the movement of people off the farms. Every indication points to the conclusion that farm people *want* to move away from agriculture when economic opportunities are better in the cities. The fundamental reason why farm incomes are low compared with nonfarm incomes is the lack of mobility of farm families. The great adjustment needed in agriculture still is to reduce the number of farmers. Yet many farm leaders and politicians talk about keeping people on the farms; they interpose blocks to action that would help improve economic opportunities for young people leaving rural areas. More about this later on. At this point I only want to emphasize the shibboleth of "rural life" as a genuine and important interference with the development of sound agricultural (and other) policies.

Parity

Oh, the sins that have been committed in the name of parity, an agricultural economist said to me wearily one day after a farm meeting. How true!

The word parity has been part of the specialized language of agricultural politics since the early 1920's. The name of the person who first used parity in the sense of a standard for prices of farm products has been lost to history. That is probably just as well, for although he could take credit for a slogan which has helped to dramatize the problems of farming in an industrial economy, he also would have to take the responsibility for some gross blunders in government price policy.

Despite its currency in public affairs over the last thirty-five years, the word parity still is poorly understood not only by city people but by farm people themselves. One trouble is that parity means several different things in the context of farm policy.

In the general sense, parity means equality of opportunity for farm people. It means roughly equal incomes for equal effort and ability in city or in country. It means opportunity to enjoy the same material level of living which city people have.

To some who use the word, parity means *absolute* equality of income between city people and farm people, without any qualifications about market values, effort, or ability. To others the only "parity" farmers are entitled to is a fair chance in a free competitive society.

Parity is used in connection with income. It is used mostly in connection with prices. It is a badly overworked word.

Every farm politician is for parity, with no ifs, ands, or buts—but you had better pin him down to how he intends to give farmers parity and what particular kind of parity he is talking about. In the 1952 campaign, Candidate Eisenhower said at Kasson, Minnesota, that he was in favor of 100-per-cent-of-parity prices for farmers. It sounded to many farmers as though he were saying he would favor legislation guaranteeing government price supports at this level. But what Mr. Eisenhower meant, apparently, was that he and his administration would work hard toward achieving 100 per cent of parity in the markets—not that they would provide this level of price support by the government.

In addition to being a general catchword indicating equality for farmers, parity also has a specific, legal meaning. It is a formula for calculating the ratio of prices of farm products to prices of things farmers buy.

Long before the government began price support operations based on a percentage of parity, the Department of Agriculture had developed an index of prices of things farmers and their families buy. This index could be used as a yardstick of farm family living and business costs. It also could be used to calculate the buying power of a given quantity of any farm product. The Department began to calculate parity prices of a long list of farm products in the 1920's. These parity prices were the prices which would give a bushel of wheat, or 100 pounds of potatoes, for example, the same exchange value as they had in some base period. The years 1910 to 1914 were taken as the base period, largely because they were the most recent years when prices were stable and unaffected by the war.

If the index of prices of things farmers buy was 160 per cent of the base period, then the price of each farm commodity would have to be 60 per cent higher than in the base period to equal parity. For example, say the price of wheat in the base period was $1.00, then the parity price of wheat under this assumption would be $1.60.

As a method of comparing price changes, the calculation of parity prices is a useful statistical device. Unfortunately, parity soon came to stand for a price farmers are entitled to receive. It came to mean a "fair" price. It was written into law by Congress as the standard to be used by the government in supporting farm prices. It also was used during wartime to some extent as a limit below which price ceilings could not be set on farm products.

Now it is ridiculous to declare that any ratio between two sets of prices is always "fair." Costs of production change. Demand changes. A ratio that is "fair" one time will be "unfair" at another time. Besides, the concept of fairness seems hardly appropriate for price relationships. The idea of equality or justice or fairness seems more appropriate in connection with income—rather than prices alone.

It is ridiculous to fix by law the ratios between prices which existed in some period in the past. But that is what the parity formula does. Whenever the parity formula is used to peg prices of farm products, this amounts to an attempt to freeze price relationships as of some base period.

The parity formula assumes that there is some "correct" or "right" ratio between farm and nonfarm prices. This assumption is irreconcilable with the American concept of a dynamic economy. Parity is a static concept and wholly in conflict with changing consumer demand, changing patterns of production, the development of new products, and with economic growth itself.

The original parity formula consisted of the price ratios of the 1910-14 period. These ratios served as good political ammunition during the 1920's and early 1930's. When the government started to use parity as a yardstick for setting prices for crop loans and other purposes, however, the weaknesses of the 1910-14 period became apparent. It became necessary to use another base period for some commodities, such as potatoes and tobacco. Also, it seemed clear in the early 30's when most farm prices were far below parity that prices never could be set at full parity. Farm politicians used parity as a sort of distant goal to talk about.

In 1938, Congress passed legislation making price supports mandatory at specified levels for basic crops. Supports were to vary between 52 and 75 per cent of parity, depending on the supply on hand and the prospects for consumption. This was the first time that Congress got into the business of setting prices on the parity scale. The levels were moderate, and the range was reasonable.

After this start, however, it was an easy transition in wartime to guarantee 85 per cent of parity, then 90 per cent, and to include a large number of the important agricultural products. For most of the war years and early postwar years these price supports caused no trouble, because market prices were far above the supports due to active domestic and foreign demand. But it was during this period that the parity shibboleth became part of the armor of farm politicians.

Nowadays no politician dares oppose parity. The Republicans, the Farm Bureau leaders, and other conservatives may talk about "flexible" price supports; they may oppose guarantees of full parity by the government. But few of them are so bold as to say parity is bunk and ought to be abandoned. They usually say, as Mr. Eisenhower said (not very clearly) at Kasson in 1952, that they are in favor of full parity "in the market place."

Parity in the market place would be just as irrational as parity achieved by government price fixing. The parity formula simply is not a good continuing standard of what price relationships should be. It is true that the old formula has been revised and is somewhat better than before. Parity prices are determined now on the basis of average relationships of the preceding ten years. The formula is constructed so that the ratio of *all* farm prices to prices of things farmers buy still is based on 1910-14 as 100 or parity. But the ratios of individual farm commodities among themselves are based on the last ten years. This changed formula takes into consideration in some measure the changing consumer demand of the last forty-five years and the changing costs of production. With all these refinements (and others, such as inclusion of taxes and wages in the index of prices of things farmers buy), the parity formula remains a crude attempt to iron a fixed set of price relationships into a dynamic market system. No matter how wise and skillful the statisticians may be, they never can devise a formula that will not go out of date. The obvious fault with the new method of calculating parity, of course, is that it perpetuates price relationships which were established by price supports based on parity. In other words, the formula simply extends itself into the future. Parity prices of individual commodities are likely to become more and more unrealistic as time goes on.

In actual operation, both Congress and the Department of Agriculture have been forced to recognize the inadequacies of parity—by setting prices below full parity. If parity were truly the "correct" price, then why should Congress not guarantee all farm prices at full parity? Although some politicians talk as if parity were a perfect standard, in practice no one seriously expects it to be carried out all the way. It should be noted, though, that the idea that the government can develop a correct formula for setting prices has been growing in recent years.

At the end of World War II both major political parties and the leaders of the major farm organizations were agreed that the parity standard would have to be revised. They also agreed that price supports should not be continued at a fixed percentage of parity as during the war. "Postwar planning" reports on agricultural policy by the Department of Agriculture, the Congressional Agriculture Committees, the land grant colleges, the farm organizations, and other research groups stated that the formula should be modernized and that price supports should be set at variable percentages of parity. This was implicit recognition that the parity price ratios were imperfect guides to price policy.

But in the fifties this unanimity dissolved. The Farm Bureau and the Republicans stuck to their guns, generally speaking, on "flexibility" and a new parity formula. The Farmers Union and the Democrats recanted. They hoisted the banner of parity to the top of the flagstaff again—or at least 90 per cent of the way. And they began to resist the switch-over to the new formula which lowered the parity prices of wheat and corn.

In the presidential campaign of 1952, the Congressional campaign of 1954, and the presidential campaign of 1956, "90 per cent" and "flexibility" became the great agricultural issues. As farm income began to sag after 1951, 90 per cent of parity came to be a symbol of sympathy or friendliness for farmers in many areas. Many candidates for office who had accepted the logic of a flexible system of price support felt compelled to join the 90 per cent bandwagon. Thus an emotional slogan superseded reason as it does so many times in politics.

In a way, however, the logic of the "90 per centers" and the full parity advocates is inescapable. Once you accept the parity formula as a measure of fairness or justice, there is no place to stop except at 100 per cent of justice. The weakness of the flexible support position is that it seems to be acquiescing in something less than equality for farmers.

This is a direct consequence of the worship of the symbol parity.

The "Middleman"

As sure as night follows day, whenever prices of farm products drop markedly a hue and cry will be raised that the "middleman" is the villain. The buyers, processors, haulers, and merchandisers of farm products are sure to "catch it" from farmers, farm organizations, and politicians appealing for farm votes. I have never worked out a statistical correlation for this phenomenon, but I am sure a "fever index" of farm protests about the middleman would shoot up with any sharp decline in the index of prices of farm products. The correlation would be especially close between downturns in livestock prices and complaints about the packing industry. This probably is because the farmer feels so helpless and so much at the mercy of the big packers when he gets ready to sell meat animals. He is in no position to bargain; he takes what is offered.

Most of the big protest movements in American agriculture have been at least partly aimed at the processors and distributors of farm products. The Grangers of the nineteenth century fought the packers, the grain trade, the railroads, and "the interests" in general. This has gone on ever since, whenever hard times have hit farmers. It has long been standing operating procedure for politicians to express alarm at the declining share of the consumer's food dollar going to farmers. Conservatives are likely to put the blame on labor and attribute the "squeeze" on farmers to wage increases which account for a large part of the cost of transporting and distributing farm products. Liberals are more likely to point fingers at profits of the big agricultural processors and the railroads. As with the other shibboleths of farm politics, there is something for everybody in this one about the middleman.

And, as with the other shibboleths, there is some basis for the complaints. Most of the businesses dealing in farm products are able to maintain fixed margins and to pass a decline in consumer spending back to producers of the raw materials. Meat packers buy hogs, for example, on the basis of the wholesale price of pork. If wholesale pork prices go down, the packers do not have to slice their returns; they simply lower their buying price for hogs. The charges made by railroads, truckers, and other transporters of farm products do not decline when prices of food products decline.

What farm groups often forget is that the fixed charges of food processors and distributors do not go up when prices of food go up, either—at least not as rapidly. In times of high prices of farm products, the farmer's share of the consumer's food dollar is high. What we have here is a set of "sticky" middlemen's charges between the producer and the consumer.

The competition among transportation agencies, among packers, among grain buyers, and among workers in these industries is not the same kind of free competition that exists among farmers. Packing companies may compete vigorously in advertising and selling, but they do not compete in the same way in the buying of livestock. This may be inferred from the fact that the shares of the total livestock marketings bought by the major packers hold virtually constant year after year at key buying points.

Because of this imperfect competition among the big processors of farm products it is probably a good thing that farm groups constantly harass them with charges of "monopoly" and "squeezing the farmer." These protests occasionally lead to government investigations and anti-trust suits, or, in the case of the railroads, to adjustments in rates. Since free competition cannot be relied upon to prevent exploitation of the farmer in the charges for handling his products, government surveillance remains the only recourse.

But farmers need to understand that they cannot expect the same flexibility in the charges of "middlemen" as in their own prices. No matter how efficient the packing industry might become, it could not operate in such a way as to take up the slack when consumer spending dropped off. The costs of a packing firm other than the costs of raw material (live-stock) are mostly fixed. It has a contract with a labor union for a fixed wage rate; its taxes are only partly flexible; its buildings and plant costs are fixed. This would be the same whether the government operated the industry or whether a farmers' cooperative did it, as farm groups have sometimes suggested.

The gains that farmers can expect from improving efficiency in the manufacture and distribution of food products are long-run gains. Short-run gains that would offset declines in prices of farm products simply are not in the cards. Politicians who attempt to put the blame on the middleman for sudden drops in prices are not being completely candid.

One reason why the middleman makes a good "goat" for any farm politician is that many of the processors and handlers of farm products are huge corporations. And bigness always is vulnerable politically. The farmer seems to be at the mercy of the "big interests." In a way he is, since he has no power to set his prices as the big firms and unions do.

But another way to look at the proposition is that the middleman is selling services which have no bearing on the price the farmer receives. The middleman is interested in selling his services at as high a price as possible, no matter what the costs of raw farm products are. The profits of the food-marketing firms seem to be more related to general economic conditions than to prices of farm products specifically. For example, profits of these firms climbed upward from the end of World War II to 1955, during periods of both rising farm prices and declining farm prices. Profits as a percentage of sales and as a percentage of stockholders' equity, however, declined from a peak in 1946 to 1955.

The picture of changes in marketing margins for food is somewhat confused by the long-run trend in consumer buying habits. People have been demanding more and more processing and packaging with their food products. The industrial boom of the forties and fifties took more women out of the home into factory and other jobs. This decreased the supply of domestic help and put a great premium on food packaging and processing for quick, easy meal preparation by housewives with outside jobs.

The middleman can hardly be blamed for the fact that the farmer's share of total food spending has gone down. People simply are spending more for other goods and services associated with food. As the economy grows richer, people tend to spend more for all kinds of manufactured goods, services, and material conveniences generally. They do not increase spending so rapidly for food itself.

Improvements in processing and marketing efficiency have been rather substantial in the last thirty years, despite the imperfect price competition among food processors. The percentage of the consumer's food dollar returned to farmers averaged about the same in 1955 as it did in the 1920-29 period. The average percentage for 1950-55 was considerably higher than in the 20's. Yet the amount of packaging and services included in food expenditures has risen considerably in the intervening years. The introduction of supermarkets in the grocery field seems to be at least one of the reasons why it has been possible to supply consumers with additional services at no increase in the share going to marketing agencies.

In the long run, however, the farmer's share is likely to decline gradually as more and more nonfood goods and services are sold with food. From 1947, the peak of the postwar resurgence in consumer spending for food, to 1955, the percentage of total consumer income going for food products held steady at around 25 or 26. Yet the percentage of income that represented a fixed quantity of the same kinds of food declined from 21 to 17. In other words, "food" spending held up largely because this included more services than before.

In marketing their products, farmers are up against the hard facts of modern economic organization. The charges for marketing are rigid, they are set by administrative decision, they are not subject to the automatic controls of free markets, such as those in which farmers must sell. Moreover, farmers must face the fact that demand for food is relatively inelastic, so consumers tend to spend increases in income for nonfood items (including food services) rather than for food.

So merely berating the middleman and charging him with the blame for declines in prices of farm products is not very helpful. Farm groups are wiser to seek continually for ways to force improvement in efficiency in marketing—by means of cooperative bargaining and cooperative competition in food processing, by means of government "watchdog" operations. The gains from these kinds of action will be slow and small. They will not prevent sharp changes in prices of farm products.

* * * *

In this chapter I have discussed at some length four of the major items of folklore about American agriculture

which have become political shibboleths. Here are three
others for brief mention (the list could be extended much
further):

"Keep agriculture out of politics." Any pressure group
tries to get both major parties and other leading interest
groups on its side. But farm groups have been unusually
diverted by the siren song of "keeping out of politics." This
is almost like saying, "Keep politics out of politics." Agricultural affairs, like labor relations, the tariff, and all other
matters of economic policy, are the very stuff of politics.
You can no more keep agricultural policy out of partisan
political debate than you can keep military policy out of
partisan politics. Agricultural affairs *are* matters where opin-
ions differ. National policy on some aspects of agricultural
policy, such as soil conservation, may achieve a high degree
of unity—just as in the case of national defense. But there
will always be partisan differences, and there *should* be in a
democracy.

"Natural foods are better than 'synthetic' proteins and
fats." Therefore, it is morally wrong to permit oleomargarine
or vegetable shortenings to be sold in free competition with
butter and lard. This idea has been and still is a force of
great influence in agricultural policy. The "cocoanut cow"
is a slogan of contempt which still has currency in Congress
and state legislatures. Mountains of scientific research have
been able only to dent this concept. It is an emotional factor
that colors much farm thinking, so, like the other shibboleths, it lends itself to demagoguery.

"Agriculture is our most fundamental industry." According to this view, agriculture is the foundation for our entire
economic system. The idea is reflected in the inscription on
the seal of the United States Department of Agriculture
which reads "Agriculture is the Foundation of Manufacture
and Commerce."

Farm organizations and politicians have used this emotional concept of agricultural fundamentalism as a weapon to obtain special treatment by government for agriculture. The more extreme fundamentalists believe that farming should be preserved and protected in its present size and organization. Such a status quo policy cannot be reconciled with the history of economic development. In 1820 more than 70 per cent of the American labor force was in agriculture, and in 1950 only about 15 per cent. The whole process of economic growth is one of making agriculture *less* fundamental in the economic system. The fewer people the nation needs to employ in the production of food and fiber, the better off it is—and the better off farm people are.

Farm leaders often try to show that agriculture is the core of the economic system because it produces raw materials which many other industries buy, sell, process, transport, preserve for storage, and prepare for eating in restaurants and hotels. Estimates of the number of people thus "dependent" on farming go as high as 40 per cent of the population. This gives a false picture of dependence on agriculture. By the same process, one could show that perhaps half the people in the country are dependent on the iron ore miners of northern Minnesota, since so much of our manufacturing and other business is related to steel.

Of course, if farmers stopped producing, the people who handle their products would be out of jobs. But farmers will not quit producing. They cannot, because then they would not have a livelihood. The people who handle agricultural products are not dependent on prosperity in agriculture. On the contrary, most of them profit more when the supplies of agricultural products are large, prices low, and farm incomes low. The people who are affected by agricultural prosperity or depression are those who sell to farmers, and since farmers have only about 7 or 8 per cent of the buying power of the nation, they cannot be a big factor in total national prosperity.

Talk about agriculture being more fundamental than other industries only blurs the facts and puts barriers in the way of enlightened farm policies.

What are the economic facts about "the farm problem"? In the next chapter we will begin to explore them.

3

A Sick Industry

American agriculture in the third quarter of the twentieth century continues to be a relatively sick industry as compared with the rest of this remarkably healthy economy.

Some people will dispute that, including some farm people. They will say the farmer is "doing all right": Doesn't he get a new car every year or so? Doesn't he have a television set? Didn't he make huge profits during the war? These common observations are accurate—as far as they go. *Some* American farmers *are* doing very well, indeed. But if you look at all of American agriculture as one industry—considered as such it is the largest in the country*—then you must conclude that it is a depressed industry. It does not measure up to the general American standard.

Average income per person largely dependent on agriculture for his living falls considerably below the average for the nation as a whole. In most recent years, according to the figures of the United States Departments of Agriculture and Commerce, per capita farm income has been about half of per capita nonfarm income. All the income received by farm people is included—for example, food and fuel produced and consumed at home, and incidental income received by members of farm families for off-farm work. In 1954 and 1955, nonfarm incomes averaged about $1,800 per person per year but farm income per person averaged about $900.

Because they have lower incomes on the average, farm people are less able to buy the things and the services which we lump together in the phrase, "the American standard of

* By almost any yardstick, including number of people employed, net income, value of output, capital investment.

living." Schools are poorer in rural areas. Medical, dental, and hospital services are much less readily available and usually of a quality inferior to that available in cities. Even such an ordinary convenience as the telephone is not available in many rural areas, and frequently the telephone service is poor where it does exist. Take any modern home convenience you wish, central heating, running water inside the home, or inside toilets, and you will find the average availability far lower on farms than in the cities.

This situation is not new. Farm people always have had lower incomes on the average than nonfarm people. Since the beginnings of civilization, people have been moving out of agriculture into other kinds of work, attracted by better living conditions and higher incomes. In the last quarter-century or so, American farm people have vastly improved their relative income status. American farmers are "better off" in relation to urban dwellers, perhaps, than farmers of any other country at any time in history.

Then why call agriculture a sick industry?

The label is justified partly because of modern ideas about income equality. The nonmonetary rewards of farming are not held in as high esteem as they once were. Farm people are not willing to put up with the traditional disparity between farm and nonfarm incomes, and the society as a whole tends to agree with this view. There has been a great levelling of incomes in the United States in the last thirty-five or forty years. The system of regulated private capitalism which has evolved here has shown far greater capacity for spreading the fruits of production among all the people than systems of doctrinaire socialism. The very foundation of the radical attacks on capitalism has been undermined by this remarkable "sharing of the wealth" in America. (The same trend has been evident, of course, in other advanced capitalistic democracies, notably in the British Commonwealth and Scandinavia.) In this climate of greater equality, economic and social, the traditional underdog position of agriculture is unacceptable.

A test of economic advancement for any country is how large a proportion of the labor force is used in agriculture— or the proportion of the total national product that is devoted to food. The fewer resources a country needs to employ in acquiring a good diet for its citizens, the more it can use for the luxuries of life—better homes, art, music, leisure, and other amenities.

Economic progress can be measured in most countries by determining how rapidly people are moving out of agriculture into other occupations. The United States has been making great progress in this respect since about 1910. The number of people employed in farming rose steadily from colonial days to 1910, even though the proportion was declining, as wave upon wave of new immigrants from Europe populated the continent. Since 1910 the number of people engaged in farming has fallen off rapidly. In 1955 we had about the same number of people employed in agriculture as we did in 1870—roughly 8 million. Yet the total population of the country rose from about 40 million in 1870 to 165 million in 1955.

How long this process of moving people out of agriculture into other occupations will go on no one can say. Great Britain in the last part of the nineteenth century and early part of the twentieth went much further than this country has gone. (She has now returned part way as a result of food import difficulties in two wars.) Britain not only reduced the number of people in agriculture but also reduced agricultural production, because in the special world trade situation of the late nineteenth century she was able to buy food more cheaply overseas. The world trade situation is different now, but even if a considerable degree of trade freedom were to be achieved, the United States could not afford to take proportionally as many people out of farming as Great

Britain did seventy-five years ago. American agriculture, a large part of it at least, has become so efficient that the gain in the total productivity of the economy from transferring people to other occupations has greatly diminished.

Nevertheless, the United States should move many more people out of agriculture from the viewpoint of maximizing total national economic efficiency. That is the fundamental reason why agriculture is still a sick industry. In plain language, there are just too many people to divide up the income which the American economic system allocates to food producers. The real solution to the farm problem of the United States, then, is to transfer people out of farming into other occupations at an even faster rate than at present. This means finding jobs for them in nonfarm work. It means keeping the economy as a whole growing and preventing relapses or even stagnation. The great depression of the thirties halted the flow of farm people to the cities. Agriculture thus, in a sense, served as a shock absorber for the whole economy. Unemployment would have been much larger in the early thirties if agriculture had not taken up some of the slack. In a much milder way, agriculture bore the brunt of industrial recessions in 1949 and 1953-54. In these years, new jobs for young farm people were not opening up in the cities, so they had to stay on the farms.

The problem of excess population on the farms is highly complicated. It is not a general problem but one that tends to be concentrated in certain areas. (More about that in a later chapter.) But surplus population is not the only reason for a "farm problem" in the United States.

Two other fundamental reasons account for the disparity between farm and nonfarm income, hamper agricultural adjustment, and help create "the farm problem." These are, first, the nature of the pricing and marketing mechanisms in agriculture, and, second, the tendency of agriculture to overproduce in relation to demand.

CHART 3. U.S. Farm Population

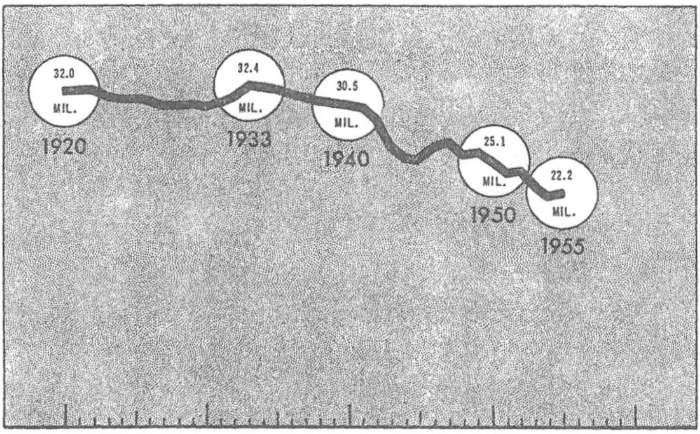

32.0 MIL.
1920

32.4 MIL.
1933

30.5 MIL.
1940

25.1 MIL.
1950

22.2 MIL.
1955

DATA FROM THE BUREAU OF THE CENSUS AND THE AGRICULTURAL MARKETING SERVICE

U. S. DEPARTMENT OF AGRICULTURE   NEG. 1825–55 (10)   AGRICULTURAL MARKETING SERVICE

Together, these two conditions make farming an extremely uncertain and risky business. Farmers not only face the hazards of uncertain and unpredictable weather, they also face an equally uncertain and unpredictable market for their products. The farmer, often hailed as the epitome of self-reliance and independence, may feel that he is at the mercy of great, imponderable forces of nature and markets which he cannot influence, any more than he can adjust his operations to their erratic changes. In his helplessness as an individual to contend with the economic forces confronting him, the farmer is almost unique in modern society. Most non-agricultural prices are set by administrative decision and enforced by the individual business firm or a trade association. If the public will not buy the goods at the price set, usually the industry can reduce its production or hold goods off the market until its price is paid, if this course of action

CHART 4. Persons Supported by One Farm Worker

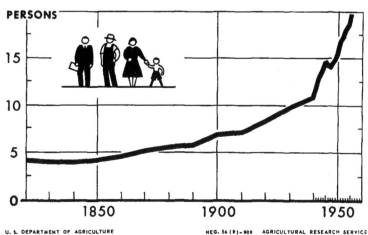

U. S. DEPARTMENT OF AGRICULTURE   NEG. 56 (9)-909   AGRICULTURAL RESEARCH SERVICE

seems to be the most profitable. The farmer does not have this kind of option. As one producer out of millions, his own entry or withdrawal from the market has no effect on prices. His only choice is to try to guess when the market will be highest and plan his marketings accordingly.

Almost everybody these days has some sort of assurance about the returns he will get for his work. A factory worker usually has the protection of a contract between his union and the management. His wages are assured months in advance, most of the time. The risk of unemployment is growing smaller year by year, because business management, labor union leadership, and the government all are learning how to adapt their policies to maintain stable economic activity. Since the end of World War II we have had two minor recessions, the second one smaller than the first, and there is every reason to believe that the stabilization record will be even better in the future. Moreover, the factory worker has unemployment insurance to fall back on for at least a short time if he is thrown out of work.

Nearly everyone outside of agriculture can plan ahead with reasonable confidence in his income so long as the national economy continues to function at a high rate of activity. This is not so for the farmer. Even at a time of great national prosperity and with a reasonable expectation that general business conditions will remain favorable, the farmer engages in something of a gamble. Though the nonfarm businessman or householder or employee can protect himself against most disasters, the farmer can protect himself only to a limited degree. He can buy fire insurance, tornado insurance, hail insurance, accident insurance, and life insurance like anyone else, of course. But there is no way that he can guard against the loss of his entire crop from drought or flood. Nor can he protect himself against a drastic decline in prices.

For a number of years the government has had an experimental all-risk crop insurance program in a few counties. However, this program has not been generally available, and the results have not been such as to encourage hope for a general all-risk crop insurance program which would be actuarially sound, that is, self-financing.

The farmer may be a rugged individualist, but he is no different from the city man in his attitude toward economic uncertainty. He would like to have guaranteed prices for his products, so that his skill in production would be rewarded. In a free and uncontrolled market, a good job of farm production in one year may bring in less money than a poorer job of production the year before. It is very discouraging to a farmer to get less money, for example, for a hundred head of 220-pound hogs than he got two years earlier for seventy head of hogs of the same weight.

Prices of farm products fluctuate in wide movements from week to week, month to month, and year to year. The short-term changes come about because of the highly competitive nature of farm markets, with thousands of buyers all over the country dealing with hundreds of thousands of sellers, and erratic movements of products to market. Market information services, both private and public, have been greatly improved in the last forty years. Still, full market information is far from completely available to all buyers and sellers, and even if it were, there is no guarantee that each producer and dealer would act rationally on the basis of the market facts.

Nobody can "set" a farm commodity price and make it stick for very long, except the government itself. And even the government has a great deal of difficulty in doing this at times.

The fluctuations in prices from year to year are caused by changes in demand for farm products and by the uncontrollability of farm production. The latter is partly a matter of uncontrollable weather. It is also partly a matter of the inability of a million or more producers of any one farm commodity to act in unison. The result is that production of individual farm commodities varies sharply from year to year—and for the most part unpredictably. (Total agricultural production of all commodities is remarkably stable in the United States, because weather differences over the continent largely cancel out, and because reductions in one crop are offset by increases in others.)

These variations in production of individual farm commodities are of two general types. One is the irregular and nonrecurring type of change in production—for example, the great increases in wheat output that occurred in both World Wars, or the great decrease in cattle numbers in the severe drought years of 1934-36. The other type of change in farm production is a regular or cyclical change. Production of most perishable farm commodities varies in cyclical fashion. Farmers harvest a big crop of cabbage in one year, and prices fall. The next year they plant less land in cabbage, a short crop is harvested, and prices rise. The same sort of regular up-and-down movement in supplies is characteristic of livestock production as well. When hog prices are high in relation to corn, farmers raise a lot of pigs, which tend to bring the price of hogs down. This discourages breeding for a new pig crop, marketings fall, and prices rise. So goes the cycle.

In making adjustments to changing prices, farmers tend to overshoot the mark. If other price factors, such as demand, weather, and government action, were constant, prices of many farm products would oscillate in wider and wider arcs—because of this built-in tendency to overproduce in response to a high price and to underproduce in response to a low one.

Demand for farm products as a group and for most individual products is quite inelastic as compared with demand for nonfarm goods and services. So small changes in supplies cause big changes in prices. For example, suppose the quantity of pork available in a given period falls off by 10 per cent as compared with the previous period. Consumers, bidding against one another to maintain their accustomed "rations," will push the price of hogs up by 20 per cent or so. In the reverse situation, with supplies increasing, consumers will pay little more to get more than their usual quantities, with the result that prices will fall sharply.

The elasticity of demand varies considerably for different foods, of course. Elasticity is very low for such foods as bread and potatoes; it is much higher for milk, eggs, meat, vegetables, and fruit but still sufficiently inelastic that a given percentage change in supply usually brings about a larger percentage change in price.

Because of the nature of the demand for food, a big crop often sells for less money than a small one (the price per unit drops enough to more than offset the larger quantity sold).

If excess production brings less income, it would seem logical for farmers to keep production down. Even if gross income were not increased, the cost of producing a smaller crop would be less and net income would be higher. But the trouble is that from the viewpoint of the individual farmer, the only way he can increase his income is to increase his production. He cannot "set" his price up. The only variable he can regulate is his output. But if enough other farmers do the same thing, total production rises and total income goes down.

Fortunately for the rest of society, farmers are unable to centralize their decision making, so as to keep production down and prices up. If they could operate as a monopoly, they could exact heavy tribute from the cities because of the inelastic demand for their products. Instead, despite government acreage controls, there is a constant pressure to expand farm production. In the United States the state of the agricultural arts is such that the supply of farm products grows at a slightly faster rate than the demand. Except during wartime, therefore, prices of farm products tend to drift gradually downward (in the absence of government price-supporting operations). Though this is a comfortable and reassuring situation for consumers, it is not so pleasant for farmers.

Farmers and farm organizations generally have been inflationists in their approach to economic policy issues. From the time of Andrew Jackson, through the Greenbacker and Populist movements, to the Farmer's Holiday and Parity for Agriculture drives of our own time, farmers have agitated for higher prices and lower production. The reasons for these pressures are based on economic fact and experience.

Farm operators have heavy investments in land, buildings, and equipment. A gradually falling price level works great hardship on owners of capital and debtors. In order to meet interest and principal payments, farmers throughout our national history (except in wartime) have been forced repeatedly to cut family living expenses. The return to the farmer for his labor and management is a residual item after fixed costs are met. Even when the general price level holds steady, prices of farm products tend to slip downhill, because of agriculture's propensity to overproduce.

A young farmer starting out today faces a steadily tightening squeeze on his returns, unless war should break out, or unless the government acts to support demand for farm products. This was the history of farming during the long period between the Civil War and the end of the century and from 1920 to 1940. The years from 1900 to 1914 were about the only peacetime period when farming was benefiting from rising prices and an advantage in the terms of trade with the nonfarm population. Exports of farm products were booming then and the United States was industrializing very rapidly. We now are well into another period when farmers will be under financial pressure because of lower prices for the things they sell and steady to higher prices for the things they buy.

Farmers are unable, as a group, to retain the benefits of their increased productivity for themselves in any large degree, and instead pass these benefits along to consumers in the form of lower prices. The classical English economists (Smith, Ricardo, Mill, et al.) thought that the free market system and atomistic competition would result in gradually rising prices of farm products as population grew and as industrial progress occurred. In the United States it has not worked that way.

The free market in agriculture has seemed to place obstacles in the way of sound adjustment of the farming industry. In an economic system where atomistic competition was the rule, rather than the exception, agriculture might be able to maintain parity of income per person. In the managed and

administered economic system of the twentieth century, however, farmers are at a disadvantage with an anachronistic
price and market mechanism, and with several million individual enterprisers making production decisions independ-
ently of one another.

Agriculture, one of the few major industries where free
competition of small producers prevails, is also one of the
few industries afflicted with chronic maladjustment in production and in the use of productive resources—especially
labor. (Another industry which has had similar trouble is
coal.) One would think that the complete freedom of choice
of consumers and the complete freedom of choice of producers would result in the automatic and quick achievement of
balance between production and consumption. One would
think that agriculture would be the *best*-adjusted industry
in the United States.

But it is not. That is the "why" of the farm problem.

The various experiments in government farm programs
all have been efforts to achieve better adjustment of agriculture. They have been aimed toward returning to farmers
a larger share of the rewards for improving productivity,
and toward getting a more efficient use of labor in farming.

There have been some results. Price supports by government buying and lending operations have introduced a
measure of stability into some farm markets. Farmers have
been protected against drastic losses of income as a result of
big crops or sudden dips in domestic or foreign demand. Yet
the basic problem of agricultural adjustment remains.

How can the farming industry meet the needs of a growing population for better diets and still maintain per capita
income comparable with that of the rest of the community?

There are no cut and dried answers to that question. But
the best way to find *approaches* to answers is to examine the
size and shape of the farming industry and the farm population, and to view them in the setting of the "new economy"
of the post-World War II years.

4

All Kinds of Farms and Farmers

All farmers are not in the same business. That is so obvious it may seem fatuous. But it is a fact that needs repeated emphasis, nevertheless. It often is ignored in discussions of farm policy. Most people talk about "the farmer" as if all farmers had the same problems.

But "the farmer" simply does not exist. There are tobacco farmers (many different kinds), sugar farmers (beet and cane), fruit farmers (you make the list), hog farmers, dairy farmers, etc., etc. The business of a New York milk producer is no more like the business of a Louisiana rice grower than it is like that of a drugstore operator. The dairyman and the rice grower are both in agriculture by definition, but they present entirely different problems of national policy.

Besides being highly diverse in kind of product sold, agriculture also is highly diverse in the commercial character of individual units or firms. It includes some people who are not really in the farming business at all.

I am one of those "farmers" who are not in the farm business. My family and I live on a 20-acre "farm" west of Des Moines, Iowa. We rent out a 15-acre field on shares to neighboring farmers for corn or soybeans. We have a couple of calves on our pasture and are producing our own beef. We have plenty of space for chickens if we should decide to take on that extra work. We have a big vegetable garden and some fruit. But the "farm" to us is mainly a place to live. We do not depend on it for income.

Yet we Soths clutter up the agricultural statistics. We add a minute amount to the commercial supply of farm products. We are one of thousands of "residential farm families" who are not really part of any national farm economic problem. We only complicate the real farmers' problems.

American agriculture also includes various degrees of part-time farm families. It includes families that produce mostly for their own use and families that produce nothing for their own use and sell everything they grow. It includes a bewildering variety of farm business set-ups. There are farmers who are really *processors* of raw materials in the same sense that industrial manufacturers are. Among these are the producers of broiler chickens who buy all their chicks and buy all their feed. Some cattle feeders around the big livestock markets operate the same way. Land is not an important factor in the operations of these processors or finishers. They are farmers but they are not primary producers. American agriculture also includes all shades of mechanization and use of mechanical power. Some truck crop producers depend heavily on hand labor, because machines have not yet been invented to handle the meticulous weeding and picking operations involved. A good many farmers, many more than we like to admit when we talk about the great technological advances in American agriculture, still farm the way their grandfathers did back in the nineteenth century. Others, such as the wheat growers in the Great Plains, have completely revolutionized production methods in the last thirty-five years.

Plainly, one cannot safely generalize about many aspects of farming in America. Farming is not like the steel industry or the electric power industry or the textile industry. These are relatively homogeneous, even though individual firms vary considerably in size. Agriculture is not even as homogeneous as the grocery business, a business that has many different sizes and kinds of firms. That is why sweeping national farm plans usually look ridiculous when you try to apply them to individual farms and individual farm families.

In order to develop sound national agricultural policy,

the policy makers (which means all of us) must understand the vast heterogeneity of American agriculture. We must understand the many different industries that together add up to the American farming industry.

The first thing to get in mind is the enormous number of individual firms—that is, separate business enterprises—in agriculture. Look at these figures from United States Department of Commerce reports. They are for the years 1953 and 1954.

Industry	Number of Firms
Agriculture	4,782,000
Retail trade	1,864,000
Service industries	740,000
Contract construction	434,000
Finance, insurance, and real estate	338,000
Manufacturing	328,000
Wholesale trade	285,000
Transportation, communication, and other utilities	186,000
Mining and quarrying	38,000

These figures in themselves suggest the difference in economic organization between agriculture and other industries. Farming still retains about the same economic organization it had in colonial days, whereas most other industries have developed large-scale units with many hired employees who do not characteristically share in the ownership of the firm for which they work. Of course, there are many small enterprises in retail trade, service firms such as barber shops and even manufacturing firms. But this form can almost be called the exception outside agriculture. The great majority of people in nonfarm occupations are working for someone else for a wage or salary. The great majority of people in agriculture are self-employed, risk-taking business enterprisers.

A very large proportion, practically all, in fact, of America's 4.8 million farms are "family-type" farms. By family-type farm I mean a farm where the bulk of the labor is supplied by the operator and his family. I would include as a family-type farm one which has a permanent hired man, even if he is married and the farm thus actually has two families. (This "two-family farm" has become more common in the Midwest in recent years of scarce labor. Farmers have been unable to depend on hiring occasional help.)

For years people have been predicting the development of corporation farming with very large units. Some have predicted the growth of large cooperative farms. Others have said that collective farming of some other type was inevitable in America. But the facts show that the family farm, instead of fading out of the picture, has been growing stronger than ever.

Of the 4.8 million farms found by the census in 1954, 3.3 million were classified as "commercial." The other 1.5 million, the "noncommercial" farms, are mainly part-time and residential farms which account for only about 2.5 per cent

CHART 5 Farm Income and Population

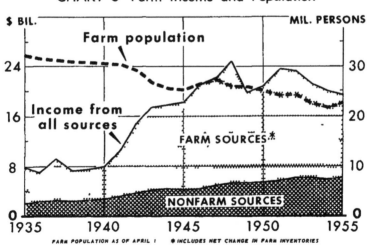

U S. DEPARTMENT OF AGRICULTURE   NEG 1519-56 (10) AGRICULTURAL MARKETING SERVICE

of the value of farm products sold. Obviously the noncommercial farms are nearly all family-type farms and mostly small units.

The census divided the commercial farm group into three main classes: large-scale, family-scale, and small-scale. Large-scale farms included all those with sales of $25,000 or more in 1954; the family-scale were those with $1,200 to $25,000; and the small-scale were those with between $250 and $1,200.

Nearly 80 per cent of all the commercial farms were of the family-scale size. But many of the so-called "large-scale" farms really are family-type farms. In nearly all cases they are family concerns, to use business language. I know personally a large number of Iowa farmers who have gross sales of $25,000 or more each year but who operate family-type farms. There were 7,228 farms in Iowa in 1950 with sales of $25,000 or more. Probably 95 per cent of these were family farms. From the census data and other information, it is safe to say that well over 90 per cent of all the farms in America are family-type farms.

For general farming, with a diversified crop and livestock program, the family-type farm seems to be the most efficient. It is true that America has great fruit farms which use large numbers of hired laborers; it is true that some wheat ranches and cattle ranches of the West are larger than the family type; and it is true that large dairy "factories" are superseding family-type dairy farms in some areas. Nevertheless, it is still true that American agriculture is family-type agriculture.

Economists and sociologists have been debating for a long time the question whether economic efficiency should be sacrificed to maintain the family farm. The individual family enterprise has been glorified as a bulwark of democracy from the time of Jefferson on down in this country. Many are the politicians who have said the family farm must be preserved "at all costs," including efficiency of production.

But despite the dire forebodings, despite the predictions that the price support and agricultural adjustment programs would lead to "socialized" farming, the family farm does not appear to be threatened seriously in the United States. Developments in farm technology have in some instances resulted in very large-scale units and "factory farms." But this has not been significant enough to be a real factor in the total agricultural economy. One could even make a pretty convincing argument that new technology has strengthened the family farm in the Middle West and other general farming areas.

In the last thirty years new technology in the Corn Belt has enabled a family to perform a larger proportion of the labor on an average-sized farm than before. When I was a boy, nearly every farmer had to hire extra help during threshing and during corn picking. Nowadays, almost every farmer can do all his own harvesting and have time to spare. The same has been true of crop operations generally, including preparing the seed bed, planting, cultivating, and putting up hay. New technology has not replaced labor in anything like the same degree in livestock operations. Trucks have simplified feed hauling. Barn cleaners, feed conveyors, and so on have helped take some of the drudgery out of livestock chores. And of course milkers have helped cut labor time for the dairyman. These new developments, all added together, do not begin to equal the saving in time that has been achieved in the work of growing crops. But the general crop and livestock farmer in the Midwest now has more time to put on his livestock than he did before, because his crop work takes so much less time.

Since the work of handling livestock has not been reduced much by new technology, it still takes about the same number of man-hours to handle a given number of livestock. There is little, if any, advantage in very large livestock-feeding or livestock-raising operations in general farming areas. There may even be some disadvantage because of the increased danger of disease from very large aggregations of hogs or cattle. This may be one fundamental reason why family-type farming continues to be the dominant form.

From this description of family-type agriculture, we get a picture of uniformity. But this is a deceptive picture. The 3.3 million commercial farms are alike only in that most of them are family-type farms.

The designation of "commercial farm" by the census may be misleading. It means only that the families living on such farms receive all or nearly all of their income from agriculture. By the common understanding of the word commercial, many of these families do not fit that classification, because their cash sales of farm products are so small. About one-third of the nation's full-time farm families had incomes below $1,000 in 1953.* This estimate includes both money income from the sale of farm products and value of home-produced food, plus an estimated rental value of the farm house.

At the other end of the scale, the top 2 million farm families have incomes that look fairly good by urban standards. In 1953 these 2 million averaged about $5,600 in net money income.* The net money income of nonfarm families averaged slightly under $5,000.

In considering farm policies to improve incomes of farm families, it is important to make a distinction between these different groups of farmers.

One trouble with our farm policies in the United States has been that they were written largely for the higher-income commercial farmers. The top 2 million farm operators pro-

* Estimates based on census data for 1949 and price changes to 1953. Farm incomes declined from 1953 to 1956 and nonfarm incomes rose. But this comparison for the year 1953 fairly represents the situation for the 1946-56 decade.

duce about 85 per cent of all the farm products sold. The price support programs, crop adjustment programs, soil conservation programs, and most of the other government activities in behalf of agriculture have been of benefit mainly to these higher-income farmers. The reason for this is that policy usually has been written with acres of land and bushels of crops in mind. Naturally, if you are concerned about wheat acreage adjustment, you will deal only with the top farmers, whose production is important.

But farm policy should be made with *people* in mind, not just crops and acres. America has a serious problem of rural poverty on its hands. But it is not a general problem, and it is not one that will be helped by generalized programs to raise prices or adjust production.

So far we have been talking about the operators of farms—owners or renters who are the heads of farm businesses. These managers and their families also supply most of the labor on American farms. Of the 22 million people living on farms in 1955, 8 million were classified by the Department of Agriculture as farm workers, 6 million of whom were family workers. The other 2 million were hired farm hands. But probably only about 1 million hired workers were engaged in farm labor as their chief activity. At least half of the hired laborers in United States farming work at other kinds of jobs part of the year.

Moreover, very few hired farm workers regard themselves as permanent wage earners in farming. Some become farm operators; many leave for higher-pay jobs in towns and cities. Since 1930 the hired work force in agriculture has declined by more than 1 million, or approximately one-third. This is further evidence that the family-type farm is not losing out to the large-scale, "factory-type" farm.

Because the turnover of the farm labor force is so rapid, there is little group solidarity, and labor unions never have made much headway in American agriculture. Farm organi-

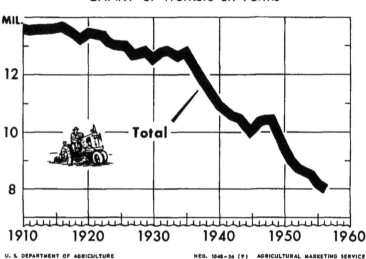

CHART 6. Workers on Farms

U. S. DEPARTMENT OF AGRICULTURE   NEG. 1048-56 (9)   AGRICULTURAL MARKETING SERVICE

zations pay relatively little attention to the problems of hired labor, understandably, for they are organizations of farm operators. Consequently, wage workers in farming are "forgotten men." Neither private nor public agencies have done much to improve their living conditions or speak up for their interests.

Farm wages average much lower than nonfarm wages, even when liberal allowances are made for housing and food provided. The reason for this is not mere lack of bargaining power but the excess of labor in agriculture. About twice as many farm boys reach working age each year as the number of farm operators who die or retire from farming. Most farm communities thus have a surplus of labor which keeps wages low. This is not a problem of exploitation of farm labor but of general adjustment of agriculture to improve technology. Better employment services in rural areas would help more young farm boys and girls to get jobs in nonfarm work and thus improve farm wages.

Perhaps a third of the total hired labor supply can be called "regular," in that it is made up of workers who stay on one farm most of the year. Wages of regular farm workers are kept low by the availability of casual labor. Many of these men are married—about two-thirds of them according to one survey. They usually hope to become farm operators and will often stay in farm work for several years in order to be available if any opportunity to rent a farm should arise.

The problems of local casual farm labor and regular farm labor cannot be separated from the over-all problem of too many people in agriculture.

Another type of farm labor, however, presents one of the most serious social and economic problems in America— even though it is small in terms of the number of people affected. This is the deplorable poverty of many migratory farm workers. The Department of Agriculture estimated that in 1952 there were about 450,000 domestic migratory workers, including children under fourteen who worked in the fields. These people worked an average of 168 days and received an average of about $900 for the entire year's work.

Migratory workers are employed mainly in California, Arizona, Florida, New Jersey, and other states which have large vegetable and fruit production. Farmers in these areas need large numbers of workers at crucial times of the year, but as soon as the harvest is in they want to get rid of the workers and their families. The employers and the communities do not usually assume any obligation for the education of workers' children, health services, or other public services. Nor do they assume the obligation to help the people to find other work.

The migratory laborer's weak position is further weakened by the importation of workers, legally and illegally, from Mexico, Puerto Rico, and Jamaica. The President's Commission on Migratory Labor reported in 1951 that "wet-backs" who cross the inadequately patrolled Mexican border are exploited by smugglers of labor, agents of employers, and labor contractors. The wetback is a fugitive and has few rights at law, so he is at the mercy of these "middlemen." Imported workers, of course, depress wages for domestic field hands. They will usually accept without protest lower pay and worse living conditions than United States workers will, because they can be turned over to immigration authorities for deportation at the will of the employer.

One of the black marks against American farm organization leaders is that so few of them have shown any concern about this situation. On the contrary, some of them have encouraged the importation of foreign labor, which makes the situation worse.

An exception is James G. Patton, president of the National Farmers Union. Patton sees the low wage levels of migratory labor as a threat to the individual family farm. In a comment on a National Planning Association report on migratory farm labor, he said: "Working farm families all over the nation are concerned that these problems be solved, because the poor incomes and low standard working conditions of migratory workers allow industrial type agricultural enterprises to compete unfairly with family farmers. Family farmers are required to sell the products of their productive efforts into the same markets where the agricultural industrialist sells. . . . I feel that industrialized farm enterprises should be required to maintain a decent American standard of wages, working conditions and living facilities for their workers. To do less is to subsidize unfair competition against more than four and one quarter million working farm families in the nation."

It is true that many fruit and vegetable farms which employ migratory labor are not carrying the full costs of their production. They do not support the farm workers during off-seasons. So the burden of this idleness is borne by the workers' families themselves and by society as a whole through public relief.

The only sensible long-run solution for the migratory labor problem is to reduce and eventually eliminate such migration. This would require the development of off-season employment opportunities in cash-crop areas that now use migratory labor. New technology may be able to reduce the peak loads for hand labor in some cases. Diversification of farming may be possible by introduction of more livestock. Probably the most hopeful prospect is the development of manufacturing and other nonfarm industries in areas that require seasonal farm labor.

It is a disgrace to the United States to allow this human exploitation to continue. Family-type farmers have a special interest in seeing that migrant farm labor is eliminated from the American scene.

5

Farmers in an Industrial Economy

During the first 200 years of settlement of the North American continent, more than nine out of ten gainfully employed persons were engaged in farming. To say it another way, it took nine farmers to produce enough surplus farm products to supply one worker in a nonfarm occupation. Farming was practically self-sufficient. The farmer and his family sold little of their production off the farm, and they bought little in town. Farming remained largely self-sufficient until about the middle of the nineteenth century.

The last 100 years of American history have seen almost a complete change in this picture. Today less than one out of ten employed persons is working in agriculture. Where colonial farmers got perhaps 90 per cent of their income directly from the farm in food to eat and clothes to wear, the top 2 million American farmers today get more than 90 per cent of their incomes in money from the sale of farm products. Even for the farm population as a whole, only about 12 to 13 per cent of total income is in the form of things consumed on the farm.

In agriculture, as in all other industries, the march of economic progress has meant more specialization and more commercialization. It has meant more marketing and more middlemen. In the early days of the last century, if a farmer sold part of his hog production, it usually was in the form of bacon, ham, or lard. He was farmer, meat packer, and grocer combined. He got 100 per cent of the consumer's dollar spent for meat. Today the farmer gets about half the consumer's dollar spent for meat. Packers, wholesalers, retailers, and transportation companies get the other half.

As farming has become more and more commercialized

over the last 100 years, farmers have become more and more subject to the general economic climate around them. Depressions and booms had relatively little meaning for farmers in pre-Civil War days. Specialized cotton and tobacco growers in the South were commercial operators, of course, and dependent on the state of general business activity and trade, especially in foreign markets. But general farmers sold very little for cash even in good times, so a cut in prices did not mean disaster.

I recognize, of course, that even in colonial days farmers were concerned about some prices, as the Whiskey Rebellion against excise taxes, to take one example, plainly showed. (This episode also reminds us how noncommercial agriculture was: whiskey was about the only cash "crop.") A drop of 50 per cent in grain prices at the time of the Whiskey Rebellion might prevent a good many farmers from buying all the gunpowder, salt, tea, and other "boughten" necessities they wanted. But it could not reduce their level of living very much, for the bulk of the family living came directly from the farm.

Today the individual farmer's income is governed in large measure by developments off the farm, over which he as an individual has virtually no control. (I am speaking here, and in this chapter generally, of the top 2 million commercial farmers, who produce 85 per cent of the farm products for sale in this country.) Nowadays a cut of 50 per cent in grain prices would put many thousands of farmers out of business. Their incomes would be reduced by considerably more than one-half, for most of their costs of production would go right on at nearly the same level. Relatively speaking, farmers are much more vulnerable to economic fluctuations than in earlier times. An industrial depression which throws large numbers of city workers out of their jobs, lowers farm incomes quickly and drastically. A change in the foreign trade situation has immediate effects on prices farmers receive.

Thus farmers have a large stake in general business conditions, the level of employment, and payrolls. Their incomes are heavily dependent on what consumers will spend for food and clothing.

What consumers will spend for farm products depends largely on how much money they are earning. The needs and desires of consumers for food and clothing do not change rapidly. Adam Smith, the early English economist and philosopher, pointed out that the human stomach does not contract or expand very much. Each of us eats about the same quantity of food year by year. Consumption of farm products is stable, but the amount of money people spend for food and clothing changes along with changes in payrolls and the national income. Gross farm income remains about the same percentage of the gross national product every year—around 7 per cent. Consumers seem to budget a rather fixed proportion of their incomes for food and clothing.

Total farm income is governed, therefore, largely by the total income received by consumers (that is, everybody) or the national income. This is a fact of very great importance to agriculture—one that has not always received adequate attention by farm organizations. If farm leaders had devoted more attention toward government action which would generate general economic recovery during the depression of the thirties, they would have accomplished more for agriculture than they did through the many special government programs for agriculture. Despite all the attempts to control production and raise farm prices in the thirties, farmers' incomes did not improve very much until defense spending and World War II revived the whole economy from 1940 onward.

Observing the close relationship between farm income and national income, farm groups sometimes have argued that prices of farm products determine the level of the *nation's* prosperity. This argument is a form of agricultural fundamentalism: since raw materials are the beginning of the processing chain, prosperity can be created simply by pegging raw material producers' incomes at a high level.

One advocate* of this point of view puts it this way: "The rest of the world needs a prosperous United States, an impossibility unless we maintain our farm price structure at a proper level so that through the seven times turn of agricultural income, we can generate the national income for national solvency. . . . Once we realize that this seven times turn of gross farm income into national income is a positive force regardless of price level, and that all groups are benefited in direct proportion by an increase of farm production and parity prices for agriculture, our problem simplifies itself. . . . The record of the United States, if properly analyzed, reveals the 'key to prosperity,' namely farm prices at parity."

Common sense quickly shows the fallacy of this line of reasoning. Practically all segments of the economy bear fixed ratios to the total. Several years ago, in an editorial in the *Des Moines Register*, I showed that the ratio of income in the fishing industry to the national income was virtually constant at 1,800 to 1. To show the absurdity of the above "key to prosperity" by means of full parity prices to farmers, the editorial facetiously advocated full parity for the fishing industry. It pointed out that fishing is at least as "basic" as agriculture. And if a "seven times turn" of farm income will create prosperity, why not an even greater multiplier?

I sometimes wonder whether the "input-output" analysts of the economy, who are so fascinated with ratios and the new electronic computers, are not abandoning reason as an analytical tool. They are more sophisticated than the "seven to one" school, to be sure. But the principle they employ is

* Carl H. Wilken, economic analyst for the Raw Materials National Council.

the same. I doubt that economic relationships are as simple as these mathematical models make them appear to be.

A dollar earned and spent by a farmer obviously is no different from a dollar earned and spent by an automobile factory worker. Each dollar spent, regardless of its source, has exactly the same influence on national business conditions. Since there are about twelve (not 7) times as many nonfarm dollars as there are farm dollars, then nonagricultural business is twelve times as important as farm business in determining national business conditions.

Agricultural fundamentalism gives a misleading view of the national economy. The nature of the farming industry is such that it cannot be a determining force in the national economy, no matter how "basic" it is. The cause and effect relationship is mostly the other way around.

The national income goes up and down with changes in industrial production and employment. Agricultural production in the aggregate changes very little from year to year. A severe drought, such as that in 1934, cuts farm output. And a united food production effort, such as was made during World War II, results in a quick increase in output. But even such changes in farm production are small. This country is so large and has so many varied climatic conditions, that droughts, floods, and insect plagues in some areas about cancel out bumper yields in other areas. Agriculture as a whole is not a variable in the United States economy. Depressions are not "farm led and farm fed" as a recent secretary of agriculture, Mr. Brannan, said. It is the manufacturing end of the production chain which creates the instability, and to identify the "villain" still more closely, it is the heavy goods or capital goods industry which has the most erratic production behavior.

Plainly, the most important way to attain farm income stability is to stabilize the national income. The most important way to increase farm income is to increase national income. All major farm organizations are well aware of agriculture's vulnerability to industrial recessions, and in recent years they have placed great emphasis on general economic stability in their presentations to the government. This is a healthy change in attitude from that of the thirties.

Both political parties, the federal bureaucracy, and the public as a whole have learned a great deal about what a modern government can do to restrain runaway, inflationary booms and runaway, deflationary recessions. The Employment Act of 1946 did not prescribe mandatory methods of preventing booms and depressions, but it set a high goal of economic policy for both the executive branch and Congress. The philosophy of the 1946 Act has been generally accepted by at least 90 per cent of the American political spectrum. It is true that the far-right reactionaries think this is dangerous "socialism," even though Senator Taft and other regular Republicans sponsored the Act; and it is true that some of the far-left radicals believe that nothing will solve economic problems except state ownership and complete government control of all industry and labor. But the great majority of Americans now agree that a modern government has the responsibility to use flexible fiscal and monetary management, along with flexible public works and other spending programs, in order to maintain the total national economy on an even keel.

Performance in line with this new philosophy of government responsibility in economic affairs has been pretty good. Since the close of the Korean war it has been superb, measured by any past standards.

Still, there remain thorny problems of instability in agriculture which are not solved even by highly skillful over-all economic management. While the general level of prices of farm products will hold quite steady during a period of national business stability (assuming no big changes in exports), prices of individual farm products may go through wide swings. Farmers can see no reason why they should not be assured reasonably steady incomes, like everybody else, and this will be a source of continuing pressure for government price stabilization programs.

It is quite possible to have a high degree of prosperity in the nonfarm part of the economy even though agriculture is in a depression. This happened during the 1920's. Many farmers had overextended themselves during World War I. Land prices were bid up to astronomical levels on the basis of wartime prices, and the mortgage debt was pyramided to a high peak. When prices of farm products collapsed after the war, farmers were unable to lower costs, particularly debt charges, and bankruptcies swept through the farming areas like wildfire. Gross farm income was fairly high during the 1920's and bore about the usual relationship to national income. But agriculture was in distress because of its top-heavy credit structure. Net farm incomes, therefore, were low, and agriculture was in a depressed state. This did not, however, have much restraining effect on the general prosperity in the cities.

A similar situation, though not nearly as severe, has developed within the last few years. Agricultural prices have dropped substantially since 1952, and farmers have suffered a considerable loss in income. Although farmers do not have burdensome debts as they did in the twenties, they have been unable to reduce costs of production in line with the fall in gross income. Despite this slump in net farm income, however, the national economy has maintained generally prosperous conditions.

Agriculture is made up of about 5 million small units, of which about 2 million are important so far as the commercial market is concerned. No individual producer can affect the market by his own operations. In agriculture we have the essential conditions of a free market economy on the producers' side. In the present-day United States economy, the farmer is the No. 1 example of true free enterprise. He has no control over either prices or aggregate production. But he is living in an economic system most of which is governed in varying degrees by administrative controls over prices, wages, and production. The American economy does not fit any textbook definition. It is not wholly an administered economy of monopolies and semimonopolies. Neither is it wholly a free-market economy in the sense that the classical economists use that term. It is partly administered and partly free.

The degree of managerial controls in different industries seems to be related in part to the size of firms in the industry. Agriculture has the smallest firms and, with exceptions for cooperative marketing associations in some fields, practically no administrative controls. Retail trade has larger firms and a few more controls. Wholesale trade runs to still larger firms and still more controls. Soft goods manufacturing marks the next step in the progression, followed by heavy goods manufacturing and construction, where prices, wages, and production levels are set exclusively by administrative decision. The number of firms at this end of the economy is small and the centers of economic power are few.

Here are some more generalizations which help describe the economy: the more perishable the product, the more competitive the market; the closer to the raw material in the production chain, the less control over prices by individual firms; goods for direct human consumption are sold in more competitive markets than capital goods. At points in the economy where administrative decisions determine prices of goods or services, there also, characteristically, wages are "administered."

This description, of course, is vastly oversimplified. But it helps show that the economy is a "mixed" economy. One gets into trouble whenever he tries to base economic policy on some sweeping theory—whether it is the theory of free competition among millions of individual businesses or whether it is the theory of oligopolistic competition (control by a few).

In an economy dominated by centralized economic decisions, agriculture tends to be a "shock absorber." Farmers' free markets are whipsawed up and down as a result of forces outside agriculture. Farmers are at a great disadvantage compared with other large economic groups in combatting business recessions. They are in somewhat the same position as a boy on the end of a game of "crack-the-whip." Small changes in business activity for the economy as a whole cause violent changes in the prices of farm products and incomes of farm people.

Why are government price supports and other farm aid programs necessary? Perhaps the best answer appears in the brief description of the American economy above: farmers are the least able of any economic group to make their own adjustments to the vicissitudes of the economic weather.

When new orders for steel fall off, the few steel manufacturing firms can reduce production, cutting their raw material and labor costs almost enough to offset the decline in gross income. Prices can be maintained at approximately their former level. This is tough on the steel workers, but the federal-state unemployment insurance program takes up some of the shock for them. The same pattern of managerial behavior shows up in varying degrees in most nonfarm business.

The chief justification for government aid to farmers is exactly the same as the justification for unemployment insurance for nonfarm workers.

If it were possible for farmers to get together to adjust their production to a decline in demand, and to maintain prices of farm products, this would be very bad medicine indeed for the rest of the economy. It would greatly intensify any business recession. If, at the time men were being thrown out of work, food prices were held up at pre-recession levels, the recession would be that much more painful for city people. Thus public programs in behalf of farmers also can be justified as a reward for maintaining full production in fair economic weather or foul.

From the viewpoint of farmers, the American price system looks unfair—it looks like a device for squeezing them. The prices of nearly everything farmers buy, whether for their home or for use in production on the farm, are characteristically administered prices and relatively inflexible. When prices of farm products go down, as a result of declining business conditions or a falling off in exports, prices of almost everything farmers buy stay up. The only element of a farmer's costs which goes down in such a period is the cost of livestock feed—something he buys from other farmers.

Now, of course, in an inflationary period, prices farmers receive rise rapidly and race ahead of prices of things farmers buy. Theoretically, agriculture gains as much from inflation as it loses in deflation. However, in the inflation of World War II, prices of farm products were held in check by price controls and rationing of some food products. This suggests another reason why agriculture has a just claim for public help during periods of depressed demand for farm products caused by reduced activity in the nonfarm sector of the economy. If farmers are denied the benefit of the full "natural" rise in prices of farm prices during a general inflation, then surely they deserve protection against the full "natural" fall of farm prices during a depression.

We hear a great deal of talk by conservative business groups about the glories of "free enterprise," initiative, and self-reliance *for farmers*. They attack government farm programs because they believe intervention in farm markets could lead to government interference with other parts of the economic system. At the same time that many of them insist on tariffs and other forms of government protection for themselves, they try to sell farmers on the idea of doing without any help from government.

As long as times are good, farmers will accept this line of talk. They *do* value independence and power to exercise freedom of choice, like everybody else. But when the choice is between unrestrained freedom with wildly fluctuating prices and some limitation on freedom with more certainty of prices, they will nearly always choose the latter. Farm people are just like other people, and they want to be able to plan ahead with reasonable certainty. In test after test the Department of Agriculture has found that farmers will choose acreage or other types of restrictions in return for a guaranteed price.

This should not shock anyone. It does not indicate that farm people are seeking handouts from the government, or that they have lost their spirit of enterprise. It merely means that they are human, and like all the rest of us, they would like to have a little less risk and a little more security.

Maybe this is really the biggest reason why government farm programs are necessary, even for the group of top commercial farmers, whose average family incomes are at least as high as those of nonfarm families. In an industrial economy of varying degrees of monopolistic and semimonopolistic controls, the only way the farmers can gain a measure of stability is through government action.

But stability is not the whole thing. In some degree, in an industrial economy such as ours, shares of the national income are determined by group bargaining or political power, rather than by free, automatic markets. Nonfarm industry and industrial labor have the power to increase their shares (as compared with the "free enterprise" sectors—mainly agriculture and small business) by raising their rates or prices. The only way farmers can get in on this bargaining act is through the centralizing power of government.

In the twenties, for a time, farm leaders thought they could establish their own monopolistic controls through co-operatives. But this did not work out well, though some special producer groups have had success in controlling output and prices. So agriculture has been forced, by the nature of the industry, to seek bargaining power through government more than other major groups.

Not that other groups do not do it also!

The whole movement for "farm relief" in the twenties began as a drive to get a "tariff equivalent" for agriculture. And even today one of the chief arguments for farm price support is that it compensates farmers for the effects of the tariff. This certainly is a valid argument for the producers of exported crops such as cotton and wheat. They can get no protection from a tariff, and tariffs on other goods limit dollar-earning imports, thus hurting their export markets.

Farmers can point to many forms of subsidy given other groups as justification for their own government aids. For example, special tax privileges to defense contractors and to the oil industry, stockpiling programs for strategic minerals which actually operate as huge price support programs for United States mines, and housing programs which help the building industry.

This is not a matter of farmers' being entitled to what others get rightly or wrongly. Subsidies to industry and business are in some measure a burden on farmers, through higher prices and higher taxes. So they feel they should get offsetting benefits, in lieu of the removal of subsidies to others. Farmers and their organizations historically fought the "trusts," the railroads, and the big processors of farm products. This attempt to whittle the big power groups down to the farmer's size, or to take away their government subsidies, now has been largely abandoned. The agrarian line of attack now is to get government subsidies to offset what cannot be taken away from others.

6

The Neglected One-Third

If your observations of American agriculture are confined to what you see along the major highways, you may be unaware of the extent of poverty in rural America today. But if you have driven on the back roads, into the hills and away from the large towns and cities, you may have seen something of the story. The rural poor are not concentrated in cramped tenements, so they do not stand out so plainly to the public view as do the city poor. Yet they form the largest single block of real poverty in the United States today, and little is being done about it.

Though you may not have seen many of these poor farm families in your automobile travel, the federal census takers have searched them out. In the 1954 agricultural census, 4.8 million United States farms were counted. The following is hard to believe, but it is true: About half a million of these farms had total sales of less than $1,200 per year, and the operators of these farms did not have enough off-farm employment—100 days per year—to be regarded as part-time farmers. In other words, these half-million farms do not include "residential" farms of city workers. The families living on these farms are the poorest people in the United States today. Some of them are existing at a level of real income not much better than that of the peasants in southern Italy and in Greece.

In the 1954 census there were 575,000 part-time farmers who sold from $250 to $2,000 worth of products in the preceding year. This group includes a good many people who are mainly urban workers and whose incomes come up to the American standard. But many poor families are included in this group also.

About 1.2 million of the 3.3 million commercial farm operators sold less than $2,500 worth of products in 1949. This means that the net family incomes were below $1,500, even allowing for some income from off-farm employment. Probably a majority of these farmers have been sinking further into debt in the last several years or have been failing to build reserves for depreciation of buildings and equipment or for maintenance of the soil. In other words, their families have been living partly on capital.

These figures I have been setting down are not from the depression years of the 1930's; they are not for some other country. They are part of the picture of United States agriculture in the boom period of the mid-twentieth century.

Where do these people live? The greater share of them are in the South. But some are in the cut-over lands of the Great Lakes states and the far Northwest and in isolated mountain areas of the West. Some are in the hilly southern fringe of the rich Corn Belt states. It is not entirely, or perhaps even importantly, a matter of poor land. Theodore W. Schultz of the University of Chicago, Kenneth Boulding of the University of Michigan, and others have pointed out that high farm income seems to be associated geographically with industrial development.

"There are strong reasons for believing that the differences in land suitable for farming, in themselves, have not been an important factor in shaping the course of our economic development. The industrial 'Ruhr' of the United States developed across the middle states to the north not because the farm land of the Corn Belt was better than that of the Cotton Belt generally, but for quite other reasons. The main effect has been the other way around, that is, the economy, essentially an independent variable, has developed in such a way as to give some farm land a comparative advantage over other land in potential adjustments to economic progress.

"This statement means that people who settled on poor land located in or near the main stream of economic development have benefited from the economic progress growing out of that development as much as have people situated on highly productive land in or near this stream. On the other hand, people who settled on good land that was located away from the centers of active development, and thus at a disadvantage in terms of making the necessary social and economic adjustments, lost ground relative to those people who settled on either poor or good land located in or near the main stream."*

Less rural poverty prevails near the large cities and near the principal industrial areas because it has been possible for farm people living there to make "the necessary social and economic adjustments." In other words, they have had the advantage of better educational systems, the opportunity for off-farm work, and the advantage of nearby markets.

Are the poor people in agriculture mostly tenants and share croppers? No, more than half of those in the lower third of the income scale own the small acreages they farm.

What are their farms like? Well, here is a typical Piedmont-region farm in North Carolina: It is a 45-acre place run by an owner-operator. The farmer has 19 acres of woodland and waste land, 2 acres of pasture, and 24 acres of crops. He has small fields of cotton, tobacco, corn, wheat, oats, and Lespedeza, 2 cows, 2 hogs, and 40 chickens. The farm takes only 180 man-days of labor per year.

Even a city dweller can tell that the farmer who runs this place has little opportunity to make a decent living for his family.

Here is a typical southern Appalachian farm: The farmer-owner has 24 acres of land to work with. He has 10½ acres in crops, including a little tobacco, 4 acres of corn, and about

* "Reflections on Poverty within Agriculture," by Theodore W. Schultz, *Journal of Political Economy*, February 1950.

6 acres in other crops. He has 1 cow, 2 hogs, and 20 chickens. The business takes 120 days of man labor.

A southern Illinois owner-operator of 120 acres has 23 acres in crops. The farmer raises 7 acres of cotton and 16 of Lespedeza. He handles 2 dairy cows, has 6 beef animals, 7 hogs, and 60 chickens. The farm is operated with 120 days of man labor.

The yearly net cash income in all three of these cases, which were selected as representative of their areas by the Department of Agriculture, would be around $500 at 1954 price levels. The farm families got about as much income in the form of food consumed at home as in cash.

This is real poverty. It is tragedy. These people are out of the stream of twentieth century American life. They do not participate in community and civic affairs. They are politically impotent. Their poverty begets more poverty. This is even truer of the rural poor than it is of the city poor, because of the former's isolation.

It is an easy "out" for the rest of us to say that these poor farmers are shiftless and incapable of doing more. It is easy for us to say that they enjoy the life they are living. It is easy to say, "Well, this is a free country. Why don't they move to bigger farms or move to the cities?" But that simply bypasses the issue. The facts are that most of the poor people on poor farms stay there. In spite of the great wave of prosperity in the last fifteen years, we still have in the neighborhood of 2 million farm families earning less than $2,000 a year who seem to be anchored to their unproductive farms.

The effects of this poverty on the farm families themselves should be enough to move a humanitarian, Christian nation to vigorous action in their behalf. But this is a social problem of such size that it concerns the rest of us in hard-fisted practical ways as well.

Clearly, the goods we all have to consume come from what we all produce. The low productivity of the poorest third of our farm families constitutes a serious burden on the nation as a whole. A Senate committee under the leadership of John Sparkman of Alabama made an exhaustive study in 1950 of underemployment in rural areas. It found a high degree of underemployment among three groups: farm operator families, nonfarm families living in rural areas, and hired wage workers who work part time or full time on farms.

"If the workers in these three groups," said the Sparkman committee, "could be employed at jobs where they would produce as much as the average worker on the medium sized commercial family farm, it would be the equivalent of adding two and a half million workers to the labor force."

Thus it is plainly in the interest of the country as a whole to find ways and means of increasing the productivity and income of the people in the lower third of agriculture—either by helping them to become more efficient farm producers or to find more productive employment outside of farming.

We, meaning the rest of us, also have a stake in solving the farming poverty problem that goes beyond mere economic interest. Democratic capitalism is on trial all over the world, and its failures loom up all the more because the total performance of private capitalism in the United States is so brilliantly successful. The weaknesses of American capitalism are measured, not by the standards of economic systems elsewhere, but by the high standards of the American economy itself.

In the matter of race relations, the United States is judged on its handling of the Negro problem. In the matter of economic performance, particularly the distribution of income, we are likely to be judged on the continued existence of large-scale poverty in rural areas. Incidentally, these two problems are related, for much of the rural poverty is among the Negro people of the South. A majority of the people of the world are both nonwhite and rural. They are keenly aware of how well their kind get along under democratic capitalism.

One of the major elements of American foreign policy today consists of technical assistance and economic aid to the people of underdeveloped areas of the world. These areas, in Asia, Africa, the Middle East, and South America, are the real battleground of the cold war of ideas. The American people widely recognize the importance of United States help to these areas to increase their productivity and achieve a better life. Public opinion polls consistently show that most Americans are in favor of "Point Four" educational and technical assistance programs.

What is not so widely recognized among Americans is the fact that we have a "Point Four problem" here at home. Senator Sparkman, who has been almost alone in Congress in pushing for action on the low farm income problem at home, had this to say in a speech in the Senate in February 1955: "I strongly support our technical assistance programs abroad. They are making us tens of thousands of grass roots friends among the peoples who have been relieved of locust plagues and the scourge of animal diseases, and have been shown new and improved methods of production. But while extending the advantages of our know-how to foreign lands, we must maintain our own nation as a showcase for democracy: the irrefutable proof that the American way is the best way ever devised by man."

It is easier to describe the low farm income problem than it is to prescribe a solution. However, it is clear that "normal economic forces" are not correcting the situation very fast. Since 1940, almost without interruption, the American economy has been operating at a high level of activity. Commercial agriculture has advanced along with the rest of the economy; farmers have paid off debts and accumulated reserves; farm families have vastly improved their mode and level of living. Yet, for reasons that are not altogether clear, in this fifteen-year boom the lower third of agriculture has remained virtually stagnant.

In the last fifteen years there has been a sort of polarization in the farm community, with the spread between the upper and lower income groups growing wider. What are the barriers which keep the low income group from advancing? The barriers are lack of education and poor schools, lack of capital and poor credit facilities, lack of technical know-how and poor communication with the progressive sector of farming, lack of opportunity for nonfarm employment and poor vocational guidance machinery.

Though the American system of democratic government and regulated private capitalism has been the most successful social organization in the world in spreading the fruits of production widely, it has not yet found a way to overcome the chronic poverty in rural areas. Most of the government agricultural programs developed during the Great Depression and modified from time to time since are of little benefit to the poor people in agriculture. The programs were designed to meet the problems of commercial agriculture. Government price supports, for example, provide little help for farmers who produce little for market. At least 1 million farm families today consume at home 75 per cent or more of their farm production, thus selling only 25 per cent of what they produce. Price support guarantees could be *doubled* without improving the incomes of these people much.

In general, the other government agricultural programs also have tended to help well-to-do farmers become more well-to-do, rather than providing a lift for the farm people who need it most. This is true of the benefit payments made during the early days of the agricultural adjustment program. It is true of conservation payments, the wartime subsidies, and most other aids to farmers. The reason for this is easy to see: the programs have been based on commercial or market production. This is not to say that price-raising programs have injured the noncommercial farmer—they just have not helped him much.

The federal government has not been wholly oblivious of the low farm income problem. In the thirties, Congress established the Farm Security Administration, which undertook to help low-income farmers enlarge their farms, obtain more capital, and increase their production. This program has been continued by Congress ever since, although the name of the agency has been changed to the Farmers Home Administration. But the program never has been very large. The major farm organizations have given it only lukewarm support. Even the Farmers Union, which claims to represent low-income farmers, usually has concentrated its attention on price supports rather than on programs to aid low-income farmers.

There can be little question but that the F.S.A.-F.H.A. approach is a sound one. This agency has had a remarkable record of rehabilitation of farm families out of the rut of poverty onto the paved highway of commercial farming and self-support.

The F.H.A. makes loans only to farmers who are unable to obtain credit from private or other public sources. Yet the repayment record on these loans compares favorably with that on private bank loans. Farm families receiving rural rehabilitation loans and production and subsistence loans from the F.S.A.-F.H.A. generally have been those at the bottom of the economic heap. Yet the principal and interest payments on these loans usually have been better than 90 per cent up to schedule.

The operating loans classed as rural rehabilitation loans were discontinued October 31, 1946. As of June 30, 1948, the administrator of the F.H.A. reported that the principal payments from the beginning of the program in 1935 amounted to 88 per cent of the matured principal. This included some of the "worst" loans imaginable, when judged by the usual criteria. Farm ownership loans by the F.H.A. show an even better repayment record. For the nation as a whole, total payments were ahead of scheduled installments as of December 31, 1954. Only about 9 per cent of the borrowers were delinquent in 1954, which does not necessarily mean that these loans will not be repaid.

The repayment record of F.H.A. loans, while impressive, is not the measure of the success of this program. The measure of success is the elevation of some farm families each year into a self-supporting status. After a few years with the F.H.A., a good many farm families become eligible for regular commercial credit. Even if there were a large government subsidy involved, it would be well worth it from the viewpoint of the general public as an investment in human resources. Actually, the subsidy is very small. Essentially, it amounts to the public contribution of supervision, education, and guidance for F.H.A. borrowers. Since many of the adults who receive educational help from the F.H.A. have not had the opportunity to attend good public schools, the "subsidy" of the F.H.A. may be considered as the "catching up" with their American birthright on education.

Conservatives often look askance at the Farmers Home Administration. Both of the Hoover Commissions on reorganization of the federal government have recommended sharp curtailment of the F.H.A. type of operation. Their attitude seems to be based on the familiar dogma about "letting private enterprise (in this case, private credit institutions) do the job." The fact that private credit institutions are not willing to do this particular job seems to escape them.

Whether the job is worth doing is another question. It is inconceivable that true believers in private capitalism could consider this job not worth doing. What is more conservative of the capitalistic system than to make private enterprisers and landowners out of people who have no stake in the economic system? What can be more conservative in the fullest meaning of the word, than to pick up the flotsam and jetsam of the American economy and restore them to full participation in the economy? Honest conservatives believe in fairness and equal opportunity for all. Is it not fair to come to the aid of those who, for one reason or another, have failed to have the equal chance of a good education?

Many critics of the F.S.A.-F.H.A. programs say that these programs are wrong because they tend to hold farm people on the land when they should be moving to the cities and getting jobs in factories. They say that agriculture's main problem is surplus people and that the movement of people off farms should be speeded up rather than slowed down. This line of criticism is typical of farm groups, especially of the American Farm Bureau Federation, which is perhaps the main reason that the F.H.A. has been kept small. The logic behind this position of farm groups, however, has demonstrable flaws in it.

The supervised credit and technical aid programs for farmers since 1935 have been too small to have had a major impact on agriculture. Nevertheless, whatever impact they have had has not slowed down the movement of farm people to the cities. In fact, the movement has been very much more rapid since these programs began than before.

It is to be noted, also, that the movement of people off farms is not just from areas of low farm income. Harsh economic conditions on the farms do not always cause people to leave and seek better employment elsewhere. The greatest stagnation of farm population is precisely in those areas where economic conditions are worst.* The movement of young

* Some evidence in 1953-54 pointed toward a more rapid emigration from the poorer farming areas to the cities. The census figures on numbers of farms in 1954 would seem to support the information on migration of people. There were 377,000 fewer commercial farms in 1954 than in 1950. This reduction can be accounted for entirely in the two lower in-

farm people to the cities is greatest from the better farming areas. Higher educational levels and more acquaintance with an urban standard of living probably are factors in this. In northern Iowa the movement off farms has been so great, and the urbanization of cultural standards so extensive, that the farm population is much nearer balance than in lower farm income areas. In some areas there are about as many people moving back to farms as moving away from them.

The F.H.A. program, instead of hindering the movement of farm people to cities, more likely accelerates this movement. It enables good farmers who are capable of managing commercial-sized operations to obtain control of the necessary land and capital to rise above the level of poverty agriculture. This process inevitably frees others not so capable in agriculture to go into other occupations. The essence of the F.H.A. program is to reduce the amount of labor used in farming.

Our attack on the low-income problem in agriculture so far has been an attack on but one side of the problem—and only a puny attack at that. It should be accompanied by a vocational education program for young farm people who want to get city jobs. Such an educational effort, if well conceived and carried out, should remove the doubts of those who think the F.H.A. keeps people down on the farm.

The fact of the matter is that no agricultural support program or aid program yet devised has had any measurable effect in "keeping them down on the farm." The results are quite the opposite. Since the farm programs began, the movement off the farms has been greater than ever. This has been during a period of rising industrial prosperity and large demands for military manpower. These off-farm factors have

---

come classes. The drop in farm income in 1954 and 1955 while nonfarm income remained at high levels undoubtedly caused many small farmers to abandon farming. It also induced many young farm people to move to city jobs.

been of far greater importance in the migration from the farms than anything which has happened on the farms.

People everywhere seem to have an "urban" standard of living as their goal—meaning modern conveniences, accessibility of cultural institutions, travel, and all the rest. The simple rural life just is not very popular, despite Thoreau and those who quote him. The pull of the city is very strong and undoubtedly would continue even at considerably higher levels of farm income.

Some cynics say the reason the important political groups in agriculture are uninterested in dealing with the low farm income problem is that they like to keep the lower third around for statistical purposes. It cannot be denied that farm pressure groups have often exploited the disparity between per capita farm income and per capita nonfarm income in behalf of price support programs. This makes an effective argument to the uninitiated. For example, in 1954, nonfarm income per capita was put by the Department of Commerce at about $1,800. Per capita farm income that same year was only about $900.

On examination, however, this disparity is quite meaningless as an argument in favor of price supports. Price supports are significant only in relation to the commercial sale of farm products. If only the 2 million farmers who produce about 85 per cent of the agricultural products for market are considered, then per capita farm income would not show this great disparity.

The real significance of the disparity in per capita farm and nonfarm income is that the lower third of American agriculture is so low that it drags all agriculture down statistically. The fact that per capita farm income is only half as large as per capita nonfarm income should be a powerful argument in favor of "Point Four at home."

Unfortunately, educators and farm leaders still do not

know a great deal about how to help southern share croppers, the uneducated hill farmers, and others in the lower third become self-supporting, commercial farmers. They have learned something from the experience of the F.H.A. and from the work of the state agricultural college Extension Services* in a few states. But much more needs to be learned about the techniques of technical aid before a really whole-sale attack on the problem can be begun. Whatever we can find out about how to rehabilitate our own low-income farm-ers would be of great value in the worldwide problem of economic development.

One of the chief barriers to action in this field has been the orientation of the Extension Services toward commercial agriculture. The Extension Services have had their chief support from the major farm organizations, especially the Farm Bureau, and consequently they have devoted their main efforts toward farm people in the upper income levels. Moreover, as any county agent can verify, there is so much useful educational work that can be done with this group that it is easy to rationalize leaving the low-income farm problem alone. Low-income farm families are more resistant to new ideas; that is one reason why they are low-income farm fam-ilies. They lack basic education and are reluctant to cooperate with public agencies—especially when they feel that the Extension Service is an "upper crust" agency.

Nevertheless, the Extension Service is a public agency. It should be available to all the people. And its limited man-power could be far more effective if directed toward those

* The Extension Services are the off-campus educational agencies in agriculture and home economics of the land grant colleges. They are co-operatively financed by the federal and state governments, with some private support. Extension work is carried on mainly through the county agent system. The county agents do much of their teaching through farm or-ganizations, home demonstration clubs, 4-H Clubs for boys and girls, rural young people's groups, and the like. (The "land grants" for state agri-cultural and mechanical colleges were set up by the Morrill Act of 1862.)

farmers who most need help. Studies by a number of rural sociologists have indicated that the higher-income farmers, those who are better educated, who have more urbanized cultural standards, are more likely to adopt new farm practices after reading about them—or after obtaining the information from an "outside" agency, such as a commercial firm or a public institution. Lower-income farmers, generally more traditional in their attitudes and less receptive to new ideas, are more likely to be convinced through personal persuasion by neighbors or friends.

It would seem wise, therefore, for Extension and other public agencies to concentrate their personal service or word-of-mouth teaching efforts on the lower income group and other "problem" groups of farmers, such as beginners. In short, the Extension Service should be doing the same job as the Farmers Home Administration, and since it is a many times larger agency, it could do a great deal more toward solving the low-income problem than the F.H.A. can.

When Extension began, in most states around the time of World War I, many farmers had to be cajoled into accepting new methods based on research. Nowadays most of the people Extension workers reach do not have to be "sold." Among the well-educated higher-income farmers, instruction about fundamentals is not needed. Extension workers are more often called upon to furnish data about specific quantities and specific grades of fertilizer for particular crops on particular soils than they are to present the case of fertilizer versus no fertilizer. What commercial farmers want, actually, is not education, but a technical service, for which they could pay as a business expense.

It is uneconomic to use valuable teaching time in meetings, demonstrations, or other individual work with the best farmers. It would be much cheaper, and equally effective, to increase the information effort through radio, publications, and television. This would release teaching manpower for work with farmers who have not yet been convinced of the value of good crop rotations, balanced animal rations, and other fundamental techniques which are accepted as a matter of course by the better operators.

Businesses that deal with farmers are doing much more educational work these days. Seed companies, fertilizer companies, meat packers, chemical manufacturers, equipment makers, and others are spending large amounts on teaching farmers improved methods. Naturally, they put their time and money on the commercial farmers who are a good market.

This is another reason why public educational agencies should focus their efforts on the lower income group. The Extension Services are duplicating services for many of the higher-income farmers which would be well taken care of by business firms, newspapers, farm journals, radio stations, farm organizations, and farm cooperatives.

Extension started as a demonstration, "show how" agency, working with small neighborhood groups. Probably this technique of teaching is still just as valid as it ever was— providing it is applied to the right group of farm people. It is wasteful, duplicatory, and unnecessary for many of the advanced farm operators to whom it is applied now.

Teaching new farm methods to farmers who are not already predisposed to change and to the value of research involves much more than just explaining a given practice to them. It seldom can be successful except as part of a reorganization plan for a whole farm, the establishing of a good record system, and training in the fundamentals of farm and home management. It is one thing to recognize that a new way of putting up hay is an improvement. It is another thing to fit this new method into the operation of a given farm.

The Farmers Home Administration has shown the value of direct, supervisory teaching with individual farm families and small groups. It has shown that adequate credit, a farm plan combined with a family living plan, and personal guidance bring improved farming.

So far the state Extension Services have only scratched the surface of this whole-farm planning method with low-income farmers. Secretary of Agriculture Ezra Benson, an old Extension man himself, is strong for the Extension idea, and he has pushed through several increases in funds for the Extension Services. He also has promoted a whole-farm planning program conducted by Extension. If this program were given real financial support, and combined with adequate credit for low-income families, the low farm income problem would be on the way to solution.

In view of its long history of close ties with the upper income groups in agriculture, however, it may be doubted that Extension is capable of carrying out the full-scale attack on low-income farming that is needed. If the Extension Services had recognized the low farm income problem and assumed responsibility for tackling it, there would have been no reason to establish an F.H.A. at all, except as a credit agency for farmers who are unable to obtain commercial credit.

Most of the state Extension Services, as arms of the state land grant colleges, do not want to have anything to do with so-called "action" programs in agriculture. They helped set up and run the early New Deal programs in the depression. But, except for some of the southern states, they soon decided that this did not jibe with their educational responsibilities. College administrators feared their institutions could not remain free to conduct research about agriculture if associated closely with the administration of government crop acreage control or subsidy programs. They would not become involved in lending money to farmers, as in the F.H.A. program. Consequently, the F.H.A. is almost a duplicate Extension Service in many ways.

If the Extension Services cannot be "rural bankers," they nevertheless can do a major part of the job of rehabilitating the lower third of agriculture. If they would really "move in" on this problem, they might regain the prestige which they had before the many new federal farm programs came in to steal the limelight.

7

Farm Education and Progress

The reader will have realized before now that the writer of these lines considers the problem of poverty in American agriculture to overshadow all other farm problems. He may also have sensed a depressing tone, a note of failure in the American agricultural economy. If this impression has been left, it needs to be corrected. Poverty in rural America *is* our number one farm problem. It *is* a striking example of failure in the American economy, but it is striking mainly because it contrasts so sharply with the progress of commercial agriculture.

If you consider only the top million and a half or two million farms, productivity per man in American agriculture averages about as high as for the nonfarm economy as a whole. It is only because the standards of the commercial segment of American agriculture are so high that the low-income problem seems so great.

In the last half-century there has been a flowering of farm technology which can be called a revolution in the same sense that we use the term Industrial Revolution. This farm revolution is not completed; it is gaining momentum as it goes along. It builds upon itself; research begets research; inventions beget inventions. Our fund of technical knowledge tends to grow in geometrical proportion.

American farmers have produced about 75 per cent more food and fiber annually during the last few years than they did in the years around 1910. This increase has come about in spite of a large reduction in the number of people working on farms. Man-hours of labor in farming dropped by 29 per cent from 1910 to 1950. At the same time the amounts of land, buildings, machinery, and other nonhuman resources used in farming increased sharply. In the latter part of this period the expansion of land area in farms has virtually stopped. But farmers have continued to use greater and greater amounts of resources from the nonfarm side of the economy: mechanical power, machines, fertilizers, other chemicals, and buildings.

In other words, agriculture has been "industrializing" very rapidly. While farm output was increasing 75 per cent, the total input of productive resources into farming was increasing only about 20 per cent.*

Let us look at this massive advance in farming productivity another way. One unit of farm input in 1950 resulted in about 45 per cent more farm output than in 1910. If farmers had used the methods of 1910 to produce the commodities turned out in 1950, the cost of production would have been something like 14 billion dollars greater than the actual cost of 30 billion dollars.

Take a shorter period. From 1940 to 1950, total output increased 26 per cent. But farmers used only about 12 per cent more units of input at the end of the decade than at the beginning. The output per unit of input, therefore, was 13 per cent larger in 1950 than in 1940. If farmers had used the methods of 1940 to produce the goods turned out in 1950, the cost would have been around 4 billion dollars greater than the actual cost of 30 billion dollars.

These figures suggest the magnitude of the advance in farm productivity in this country. The rate of growth has been about on this order: an improvement of about 1 per cent per year in output per unit of input; an improvement of about 3.5 per cent per year in output per unit of labor. This rate of increase in productivity per man fully equals the rate of increase in productivity in nonfarm occupations over the same period.

(Remember that these figures apply to agriculture as a

* Estimated by Theodore W. Schultz, *The Economic Organization of Agriculture*, McGraw-Hill, 1953.

whole and refer to all the workers in agriculture, as listed by the census. If only the 2 million top farms were considered, the rate of advance in productivity would be very much higher.)

What caused this startling rise in farm efficiency? Broadly speaking, it is the result of the application of science to agriculture. It goes hand in hand with the similar advance in nonfarm production. It has been "forced" by the pull of an expanding industrial economy for labor. The other side of this same coin is that more labor efficiency in farming has "released" manpower for use in manufacturing, distribution, and other services.

More specifically, the improvement in farm productivity has come about through the planned research of the United States Department of Agriculture and the state experiment stations, supplemented by commercial research and development, especially by farm machinery and equipment makers. The recent rapid upsurge in farm technology has coincided with the growth of the system of research and education in the U.S.D.A. and land grant colleges.

In late years we have been spending about 100 million dollars a year for agricultural research by these public institutions, and about 75 million dollars a year for teaching farmers new methods through the Extension Services.* Though we cannot attribute all the gains in production efficiency to the work of these public institutions, it is obvious that returns on public investments in research and education in agriculture have been extraordinarily large.

* All federal and state agricultural agencies are, in a broad sense, "educational" and contribute to the dissemination of new farm technology. However, the Extension Services have the major responsibility. The Soil Conservation Service, the Farmers Home Administration, the Agricultural Stabilization and Marketing Service, the Forest Service, and high school teachers of vocational agriculture make great contributions in the education field.

CHART 7. Efficiency in Use of Farm Labor

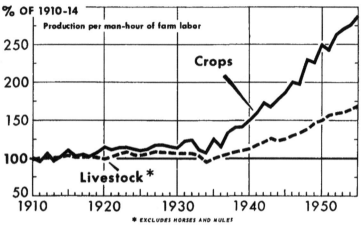

% OF 1910-14

Production per man-hour of farm labor

Crops

Livestock*

1910   1920   1930   1940   1950

* EXCLUDES HORSES AND MULES

U. S. DEPARTMENT OF AGRICULTURE   NEG. 55 (9)-919   AGRICULTURAL RESEARCH SERVICE

The public research and educational system in agriculture is indeed one of the great social inventions of the United States. It is unique in the world. No one can understand American agriculture without appreciation of the land grant college system. It has provided for a constant flow of new techniques from the laboratories and test plots to the farms. The results suggest that society could well afford to invest still more in agricultural research and education. The general public receives the benefits from advancing productivity through larger food and fiber supplies and lower prices, usually very quickly.

The land grant college system is an interesting example of federalism in a special field of public activity. Federal contributions to the state institutions are entirely in the form of grants-in-aid, with very few strings attached. Part of the funds must be matched by state appropriations. However, federal control over the state institutions has been notable for its absence.

CHART 8. Farm Labor Productivity

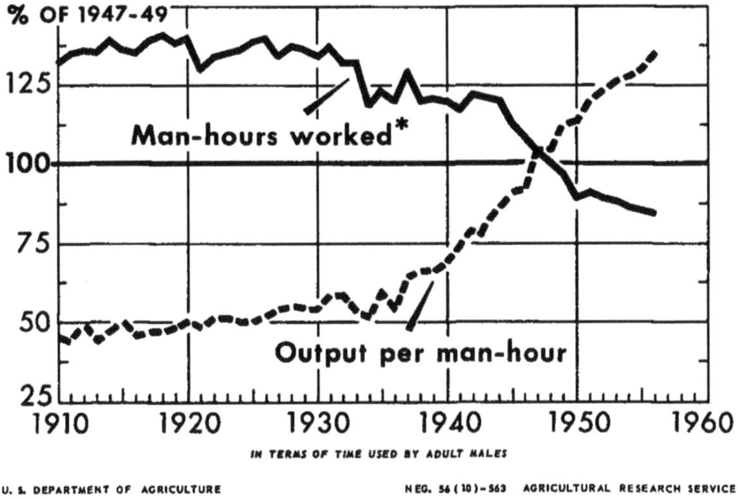

IN TERMS OF TIME USED BY ADULT MALES

U. S. DEPARTMENT OF AGRICULTURE   NEG. 56 (10)-563   AGRICULTURAL RESEARCH SERVICE

In a study of the political and governmental relationships of the land grant colleges and universities,* Charles M. Hardin found little evidence of attempts by federal farm agencies to interfere with the freedom of the colleges in research and teaching. He found still fewer examples where the attempts were successful.

As a member of the agricultural economics faculty at Iowa State College, the writer experienced some instances in which federal farm agencies, mainly the old Agricultural Adjustment Administration, tried to influence research activities of the Iowa Agricultural Experiment Station. For example, the state office of the A.A.A., backed up by regional and national officials, objected strongly to the publication of a study which indicated that corn acreage reductions in Iowa had not reduced livestock feed production but had increased it. The report was published, nevertheless.

* Charles M. Hardin, *Freedom in Agricultural Education*, University of Chicago Press, 1955.

The significant feature of clashes between the federal Department of Agriculture and its action agencies, on the one hand, and the state agricultural colleges, on the other, is that the state institutions nearly always have won. Land grant college presidents, Experiment Station directors, and Extension Service directors usually have felt strong enough politically to resist attempts by federal agencies to encroach on their freedom of scientific inquiry and education. The land grant college system effectively answers those who fear that federal grants-in-aid to public schools or colleges and universities necessarily means federal control and infringements on academic freedom.

One could make a convincing argument that the land grant college system proves the need for *more*, rather than less, federal direction. For these state institutions, despite their cooperative relationships with the national government, have been highly vulnerable over the years to state and regional political pressures and influences. Professor Hardin's study presents evidence of the pliability of the land grant college research and Extension agencies when confronted by special economic interests in their states. The celebrated "censorship" of a pamphlet on the economic problems of the dairy industry at Iowa State College in 1943 is only one of hundreds of similar incidents which have taken place in nearly all the state agricultural colleges.

In this instance the dairy groups in Iowa objected to the pamphlet largely because it said that fortified oleomargarine compared favorably with butter in nutritional value and palatability. They also objected because the pamphlet advocated a reorganization of the dairy industry to deemphasize the production of butter and to emphasize the production of whole milk for fluid consumption. That the conclusions of this piece of research were fundamentally sound seems obvious today. The economic reasoning appeared sound enough to most impartial observers of the dairy industry in 1943, for that matter. Yet the state Board of Education and the college bowed to protests by the dairy groups, withdrew the pamphlet from publication, and published a revision, correcting errors of "fact." The Board of Education even had the gall to issue a statement saying that academic freedom had not been interfered with at Iowa State College.

So far as the effects on the dairy industry and the public of this particular pamphlet are concerned, the "suppression" was supremely ineffective. The basic problem of the Iowa dairy industry probably got more public attention because of this than it ever would have otherwise. Undoubtedly, the furor over the pamphlet has contributed since then to more intelligent and less dogmatic consideration of dairy industry problems and policy in Iowa. The state legislature removed the 5-cents-per-pound tax on margarine in 1953 and also eliminated the ban against colored margarine. The ruckus of 1943 had a bearing on this action, which was relatively enlightened and relatively quick (compared with what happened in neighboring dairy states, Wisconsin and Minnesota).

But the losses which ensued from the row over the dairy pamphlet far outweighed the gains. Iowa State College lost the core of its economics faculty, which had been one of the finest in any land grant institution. It suffered heavily in reputation among scholars and educators.

(The writer was in the Army at the time of the margarine incident and the "great exodus" of agricultural economists which followed, so these comments are not those of a participant but of one who was away but fully informed of the background and the issues.)

Not many of the economic group pressures brought to bear on the land grant colleges explode like the Iowa margarine issue did. The typical situation is for the college to back away from "a hot one" rather than risk getting into trouble. The land grant colleges unquestionably benefit from their close association with general farm organizations and commodity groups. More than any institutions of higher learning in the world, the state agricultural colleges really are "close to the people." But this intimacy also leads to feelings among farm pressure groups that they "own" the college—a feeling that is not completely unwarranted.

To continue with the example of the dairy industry, the agricultural colleges of the North Central region have been "cowed" by the dairy farmers, the creamery operators, and other milk industry interests. Considering the importance of dairying to the North Central region, the state experiment stations have carried on comparatively little objective inquiry into the economic problems of the industry. There has been little analysis of the effects of vegetable oil competition with butterfat on dairy manufacturing and marketing.

The vested interests of the dairy industry have been effective in using the colleges to maintain their vested position. Even today it would take an unusually bold dean of agriculture in a dairy state to approve a report which said that butter making should be reduced still further, that oleomargarine when fortified with vitamins is just as good a food as butter, and that consumers should buy margarine instead of butter because it is cheaper. Yet these are the plain realities of the situation, as even most dairy farmers now recognize.

On the whole, however, the influence of the land grant colleges has been strongly for progress in agricultural production, processing, and marketing. Their constant drive for better technology has been much the biggest single institutional influence on American agriculture—far exceeding the influence of the federal action agencies of the last twenty-five years. The reason why the United States spends a smaller proportion of its total income for food than any other country in the world may be credited in large degree to the land grant college system of research stations and Extension Services.

The experiment stations and Extension Services in all the

states from the beginning have been geared to the interests of the better farmers, those who belong to farm organizations. This is natural. The administrators of these public institutions have to rely on public support, through the state legislatures, for financial backing. They understandably have turned to the groups which could be most effective in their behalf and were most sympathetic to their aims. Although the colleges have formed working alliances with many farm organizations, farm cooperatives, and other groups, by far the most important of these alliances is with the Farm Bureau.

The relationships between the Farm Bureau and the land grant colleges, especially their Extension Services, have affected the whole course of agricultural development, the character of the national farm action programs, and farm politics in general. The Farm Bureau has provided the land grant college system with its most vigorous and steadiest political support, both on the state and national levels. It is much the largest and the most widespread of the general farm organizations. It maintains strong legislative lobbying staffs in Washington and in most of the state capitals. During the last several years, since official reports on lobbying expenditures were first required by Congress, the Farm Bureau regularly has been among the first four or five national organizations in total amount spent in lobbying.

The state Farm Bureaus are powerful political forces in many states but especially so in the Middle West. The strongest state Farm Bureau organization from the standpoint of legislative influence is the Iowa Farm Bureau. The Iowa organization is second in size only to the Illinois Agricultural Association (state Farm Bureau). But rural Iowa is more dominant in the state legislature than rural Illinois is in the Illinois Assembly. The Iowa Farm Bureau completely overshadows other farm organizations in the state, and so maintains a commanding role in the state legislature.

Without doubt, it is far more influential than the manufacturers' association, the labor organizations, trade and professional associations, or any other group in the state.

Having the Farm Bureau generally on their side has been of great benefit to the land grant colleges. It is easy to understand why experiment stations and Extension Services have been susceptible to influence by Farm Bureau leaders.

The relationship between the Farm Bureau and the land grant college system is not just the ordinary tie-up between a public agency and a related, benefited pressure group. It is closer than that. Until recently there was an official bond between the Extension Services and the Farm Bureaus in several of the most important agricultural states. A feeling of camaraderie and joint purpose has existed among Farm Bureau and land grant college people for many years. The Farm Bureau got its start as a state and national organization by virtue of sponsorship by the Extension Services. Now it has become so large, strong, and independent that the "sponsorship" is the other way around.

The first "farm bureau" was established in Broome County, New York, in 1911. The Binghamton Chamber of Commerce in that county had an agricultural committee with some farmer members. It decided to hire a county farm adviser or educational leader and set up a farm information service, which it named the "farm bureau." A membership organization for sponsoring this work was not formed until 1913. Its first name actually was "farm improvement association," and its first president was the master of the county Grange.

The first "farm bureau association" was organized in Chemung County, New York, in 1913. In several other counties where county agents were hired in the next few years, the county agents' offices were called farm bureau offices. The county agents were called farm bureau managers. This is how the association between the words "farm bureau" and "extension" began.

In 1914, Congress passed the Smith-Lever Act providing for agricultural extension work to be carried on cooperatively by the Department of Agriculture and the state agricultural colleges. In the next several years about half the states passed laws legalizing the formation of farm bureaus or crop improvement associations to guide the Extension Services. During World War I the farm bureaus were promoted by government agencies to help expand production of food.

In these years several states formed federations of the county bureaus. The first evidences of any breaking away from strictly educational objectives came in Illinois in 1916, when the Illinois Agricultural Association voted in convention to make legislative problems the first order of business.

In 1920 the American Farm Bureau Federation was formed as a general farm organization, with political action in mind.

In 1921 a memorandum of understanding was drawn up between the federal Extension Service in the Department of Agriculture and the American Farm Bureau Federation. This agreement called for a clear separation in functions between the two agencies. The county agents were to consider themselves public servants working for all farmers, not just Farm Bureau members. They were not to solicit Farm Bureau memberships, handle dues, engage in commercial activities, or take part in other Farm Bureau activities beyond that of education. In 1922 the Association of Land Grant Colleges and Universities approved a report which said, "It is recognized that Extension workers are public officials, paid from public funds and should use their efforts in work beneficial to all." Henry C. Wallace, the secretary of agriculture under President Harding, promulgated an official code of conduct for state Extension Services based on the same general doctrine of independence from the Farm Bureau and its political and commercial activities.

These agreements and official doctrines were violated right from the start. In a great many states, county agents continued to solicit memberships for the Farm Bureau, to manage Farm Bureau business enterprises, and to take an active part in the political pressure activities of the Farm Bureau. In many states Extension work was known as Farm Bureau work, and to some degree it still is in such states as Iowa and Illinois. County agents were known as Farm Bureau agents.

The semiofficial nature of the Farm Bureau enabled it to recruit new members on the strength of advantages in connection with Extension programs, including the 4-H Club activities for boys and girls. During the depression years of the thirties other agricultural issues so far superseded the Farm Bureau–Extension tie-up that other farm organizations made relatively few protests. However, in the forties this relationship came under increasing criticism from other farm organizations and from the Department of Agriculture.

The Extension Services, which were supposedly official agencies cooperating with the federal Department of Agriculture, often refused to go along with Department of Agriculture policies. And when the Farm Bureau was at odds with the secretary of agriculture, the Extension Services were more inclined to follow the Farm Bureau than the secretary.

In the first year of World War II, for example, Agriculture Secretary Claude Wickard wanted to make use of the reserves of corn and wheat which had been built up under the price support loan programs, to expand production of livestock for war needs. To do this, he wanted to sell these reserves at less than the parity price, and he wanted to reduce loan rates to prevent further accumulation. The Farm Bureau opposed the Wickard policy. Although it has since become a strong advocate of lower and more flexible price support, the Bureau at that time was a champion of protecting the farmer's price level and maintaining price supports as high as possible.

Partly because of this conflict and similar ones, in 1941 Secretary Wickard issued a memorandum reminding state Extension officials of the 1921 agreement covering relations with a general farm organization.

Several states changed their laws or their practices about local sponsorship of Extension by the Farm Bureau.

In 1948 the Association of Land Grant Colleges and Universities made a thorough study of the Farm Bureau–Extension relationship and concluded: "It is not sound public policy for Extension to give preferred service to any farm organization, or to be in a position of being charged with such actions. . . . It would be in the public interest for any formal operating relationships between the Extension Service and any general farm organization, such as the Farm Bureau, to be discontinued at the earliest possible moment."

Since then the movement to sever the official connection between the Farm Bureau and Extension has grown to cover practically all states. Laws which provided for Farm Bureau sponsorship and control of county funds appropriated for Extension work had been discontinued in Kansas, Montana, Nevada, South Dakota, and Vermont by 1952. Laws in Missouri and Nebraska were revised to permit local sponsorship and management of county funds by any farm organization. New York State decided in 1954 to "divorce" its county Extension Services from the Farm Bureau.

In December 1954 Secretary of Agriculture Ezra Taft Benson issued a directive calling for the complete separation of the Extension Services (and other federal farm agencies) from any farm organization. But by this time, only the two stand-pat Farm Bureau states of Iowa and Illinois still retained the official tie-up. In these two states the county Farm Bureaus contributed a considerable share of the Extension budget from their own organizational funds—in Illinois about 40 per cent and in Iowa about 20 per cent. In all other states the Farm Bureau contribution, as well as contributions from other farm organizations, ranged from very small to nothing at all. Although there were many protests in Illinois and Iowa about Secretary Benson's directive, both states have gone through with the separation.

Legal separation of the Farm Bureau and the Extension Service and the complete replacement of Farm Bureau contributions to Extension salaries and expenses, will not mean a sudden change in the close association of these allies, which has existed for more than thirty-five years. So far as general agricultural policies are concerned, the Farm Bureau and the land grant colleges are likely to stand shoulder to shoulder for some time to come. This would be true regardless of their long time "marriage." The Farm Bureau is the most conservative of the general farm organizations and generally favors a minimum of federal intervention in agricultural markets and the individual farm business. As institutions the land grant colleges, like almost all colleges, tend to be conservative. Moreover, as noted earlier, the land grant colleges in many states have to depend on the Farm Bureau for political pressure in their behalf at legislative appropriation time.

In light of Farm Bureau history, it is not surprising that this organization has consistently opposed anything in the federal Department of Agriculture which appeared to open up the opportunity for a rival farm organization. For example, in the late thirties and early forties the Farm Bureau was greatly concerned about the activities of some Agricultural Adjustment Administration officials in the North Central region to mobilize political support for A.A.A. policies. The A.A.A. officials attempted to weld county A.A.A. committees into a political action organization. Or perhaps it is more accurate to say that some of them talked as though they would like to do this. Actually, this political movement of A.A.A. committees never got very far.

The Farm Bureau also has shown concern about the soil conservation district commissioners and their relationship to the federal Soil Conservation Service. And some Farm Bureau leaders apparently have viewed with alarm the county and state advisory committees of the Farmers Home Administration.

But the Farm Bureau had its biggest scare in 1938 when Secretary Henry A. Wallace reorganized the Department of Agriculture and made the Bureau of Agricultural Economics the "general agricultural program planning and economic research service for the secretary and for the department as a whole." In carrying out this assignment the B.A.E. set out to establish land use planning committees in every county. The Farm Bureau had good reason to fear that the land use planning committees could become the foundation of a new general farm organization, capitalizing on a tie-up with an official agency. Had not it done precisely the same thing? The Farm Bureau soon succeeded in knifing the land use planning program, a bit of surgery in which it had the whole-hearted cooperation of federal action program agencies which were jealous of the B.A.E.'s being strengthened and being assigned the planning function over them.

Throughout the last twenty-five years of federal action programs in agriculture, the Farm Bureau has thrown its political weight around to prevent any general farm organization from arising to challenge it. This is one reason why it has resisted the growth or increase in power of any of the federal farm agencies, sometimes attacking one, sometimes attacking another. In the tussle for federal funds, the Farm Bureau can be depended upon to take up the cudgel in behalf of the grants-in-aid to the state experiment stations and Extension Services.

Since the Farm Bureau grew up in the aura of the land

grant college system, it attracted the farm people who were progressively minded, appreciated the value of scientific research, and welcomed the advice of a county agent. The Farm Bureau membership is heaviest among the upper-income families, the more conservative element in American agriculture. They tend to oppose change and especially to be skeptical about government programs. *Relatively* skeptical, that is, for even most of the Farm Bureau members are thoroughly convinced that many of the New Deal farm programs have been worthwhile and should be maintained.

The Farm Bureau from its beginning has been a battler for more agricultural research and education. A great deal of the amazing progress of the American commercial farmer must be credited to this organization. By the same token, the Farm Bureau must bear a major share of the responsibility for the plight of the bypassed third of agriculture, which has not had much benefit from Extension adult education, 4-H Club activities, or the other public aids to agriculture.

8

The Surplus Problem

We are now ready to begin talking about ways of correcting the imbalances in commercial farming. I repeat once again that these imbalances are not the *major* farm problem in the United States. Rather, it is low income—poverty—and what we may call noncommercial agriculture. In many ways, however, rural poverty is more than a farm problem: it is a national social problem, and a national economic development problem. Rapid progress in improving the productivity of the lower third of agriculture would still leave untouched most of the annoying and discouraging maladjustments which afflict commercial farmers.

Probably no domestic issue has received more attention than the farm surplus (or low price) situation in the last thirty-five years. Except for the comparatively brief periods of wartime inflation during the 1940's and during the Korean war of 1950-51, farmers and farm groups have been agitating about low prices of farm products. It is a mistake to pass this off as nothing more than the proclivity of farmers to belly-ache. Many volumes have been written about the hardships suffered by the nation's best farmers during the twenties and thirties. The agitation for farm relief, the discontent among farm people throughout the Corn Belt and the Great Plains states were the consequences of real, not imagined, suffering. Thousands of farm families in my own state of Iowa, after years of grinding sacrifice to meet payments on mortgages, in the end lost their farms—not just during the Great Depression when virtually everybody was hard up, but even during the decade of the twenties when almost everybody except farmers was enjoying rising living standards.

The "farm depression" of the twenties was a consequence, largely, of the loss of foreign markets after World War I which sharply depressed prices. The fixed costs of agriculture had been raised to new heights during the war and shortly afterward. Land prices had climbed steeply and the mortgage debt structure had been built up in line with the inflated prices of land. So farmers were in a tight squeeze between costs (including living costs) which tended to hold near wartime levels, and prices of the things they sold which fell precipitately.

In the early twenties began the "great debate" about farm relief or government programs for agriculture—a debate that has continued down to this time and is still unsettled.

In an article for the May 1955 *Journal of Farm Economics*, Professor J. K. Galbraith of Harvard University reminded his readers that all the old farm problems still exist, in spite of strenuous efforts to solve them. He wrote:

"Farm policy has long been a serious source of discouragement to those who believe that, with thought and effort, public problems, however intractable, can be made to yield, however gradually, to solution. Such discouragement must seem deeply justified at the moment. We have just come through a notably agonizing reappraisal of our farm policy.

"First, beginning in 1953, there was a lengthy period of conference and discussion. Those whom the new administration agreeably characterized as 'the best minds' were consulted at length and called on for a program. The people in general, and the congress in particular, were promised that the result would be a new and fresh approach to this old and tired problem. The congress also made a notable effort to inform itself. Then, during the 1954 session of congress, the administration presented its proposals, and these were debated at great length. Eventually, the proposals, intact in broad outline, were enacted into law. The whole issue was then reviewed in the election campaign of 1954.

"This was a formidable effort. One is all but compelled to suppose that something important was accomplished. Herein lies the reason for the peculiar discouragement of the moment. Under the new farm bill, the country can reasonably expect to have all the troubles that afflicted it under the old one. Despite all of the effort no substantial problem of past farm policy was solved or greatly mitigated."

For more than thirty years farm organizations, the political parties, Congress, the Department of Agriculture, and a large proportion of the membership of the Farm Economic Association have been giving close attention to the problem of overproduction in agriculture. But today the problem is as far from being solved as ever. In fact, the physical quantity of agricultural surpluses towers far above any previous accumulation.

In the case of wheat, which has been the most troublesome surplus crop, the supply in reserve (as of mid-1956) amounts to more than a full year's domestic consumption and export. Despite stringent controls on acreage which have reduced the land planted to wheat by one-third in the last several years, farmers continue to grow more wheat than can be sold at home and abroad.

It *is* discouraging, as Professor Galbraith says.

In the last thirty years a good many schemes have been advocated for keeping prices of farm products up and production down, or getting rid of surpluses overseas, or using more farm food products as industrial raw material, or controlling the supply of and demand for farm products in some other way. None of these schemes has panned out very well.

In the early twenties the first major effort to deal with the low farm price problem was through cooperative marketing. Farm groups were taken with the idea that "orderly marketing" would cure their price difficulties. Legislation favorable to the organization of farm marketing cooperatives was pushed through Congress and a hectic period of organizing farm coops set in. The disillusionment with cooperative marketing as a solution for the farm surplus problem came swiftly.

Farm organizations soon turned their attention toward more aggressive government action which might protect their prices. The most important of these efforts was the one to establish a guaranteed price to farmers in the home market by dumping the surplus overseas at reduced prices. Several variations of the idea were proposed during the twenties. The McNary-Haugen Bill, which would have maintained domestic prices of basic crops at a fair "ratio-price" (the precursor of parity) by means of export dumping, came the closest to success. It passed Congress twice, in 1927 and 1928, but was vetoed by President Coolidge both times.

The McNary-Haugen plan, the "export debenture" plan, and several other variations of the idea were to be self-financing. Taxes would be collected at the point of first sale under the McNary-Haugen plan, for example, sufficient to defray the costs of sale overseas at a lower price than the guaranteed domestic price. Because of the inelastic demand for most farm products, prices would rise enough in the home market to more than offset the cost of the sale overseas. The purpose was to give the farmer a guaranteed "fair" price for all of his product consumed in the domestic market plus the world price for all sold abroad. The "fair" price was supposed to be the world price plus the tariff. The McNary-Haugen plan was advocated as a means of "making the tariff effective for agriculture."

It is worth noting that this first major effort of agricultural groups to deal with farm surpluses was essentially an isolationist or protectionist solution. Farm groups did not oppose the protective tariff on manufactures; they simply wanted to provide the benefits of tariff protection for farmers. Dr. Murray R. Benedict of the University of California says that farmers might have obtained more relief by advocating a liberal tariff policy:*

"On the score of reviving and strengthening the foreign market, it seems clear that both farm leaders and the congress misjudged the situation and chose the wrong solution. Europe was badly disorganized; Germany in the throes of inflation, France ravaged by invasion and battle and England weakened by years of fighting. Little strength could be expected in an export market so grievously disrupted. All of these nations needed dollars and were faced with the problem of reviving their industries and shipping. As soon as possible they needed to begin exporting to the United States in order to obtain dollar exchange in vital necessities. True, they were in no position to spare large quantities of goods. Yet we tended to discourage such exports as they could have made available. The emergency tariff of 1921 and the Fordney-McCumber tariff of 1922 were definitely designed to hold down imports at a time when our own economy was short of goods and our manufacturers were reaping a rich harvest by selling at high prices at an undersupplied market. In addition, we put pressure on our wartime allies to begin repayment on their vast war debts with the limited dollar exchange they had.

"The results of this policy were unfavorable to American agriculture in several ways. The European nations, who had been our best prewar customers for farm products, exerted every effort to revive their agriculture quickly in order to save dollars. They also turned to other sources of supply, such as Canada, Argentina and Australia. In the home market, the policy of shutting out foreign goods contributed to the maintenance of high prices for nonfarm products, and

* Murray R. Benedict, *Farm Policies of the United States, 1790-1950*, Twentieth Century Fund, 1953.

a continuing high level of wages, thus widening the spread between farm and nonfarm prices.

"Logically, the farm groups should have supported a continuance of the lower-level Underwood tariff. Had they done so successfully, it is conceivable that the farmers' position would have been easier in the Twenties, and that the disastrous crash of 1929 would have been delayed or made less severe, since it developed in part as a result of strain placed on foreign currencies in the effort to maintain dollar payments to the United States."

It is interesting to speculate about what course American agricultural policy might have taken had the McNary-Haugen Bill been enacted. The fact that it was not undoubtedly paved the way for more drastic government efforts to deal with farm surpluses under the New Deal in the thirties.

With the election of Herbert Hoover in the fall of 1928, a new attack on the agricultural surplus problem was launched. This was the attempt to protect prices of farm products by buying up and storing surpluses, but without any specific price guarantee and without any scheme of export dumping. The Agricultural Marketing Act of 1929 provided for a Farm Board of eight members to be appointed by the president. This board was given a revolving fund of 500 million dollars. It was authorized to make loans to farm cooperatives for effective merchandising of farm commodities, construction or acquisition of facilities, formation of clearing house associations, extending the membership of the cooperatives, and making higher advances to growers than could be provided through other credit agencies. Thus the new plan was to help the cooperatives solve the farm problem by stabilization operations.

The Farm Board had barely got organized and ready to operate when the stock market crash occurred. Not long afterward Congress passed the Hawley-Smoot Tariff Act, raising duties to all-time highs and virtually strangling United States foreign trade. The Great Depression was on its way, and it is no wonder that the efforts of the Farm Board were dismally unsuccessful. The Board established the Farmers National Grain Corporation, which tried to stabilize the price of wheat by holding grain off the market. American wheat prices probably were held above the usual relationship to world prices through late 1930 and the first half of 1931, according to Benedict. But on June 30, 1931, the Board decided to begin liquidating its holdings, because it did not feel that its resources permitted it to go any further. It held 257 million bushels of wheat—which would seem a very moderate carry-over today.

As a result of the miscarriage of the federal Farm Board price stabilization efforts, agricultural leaders looked with favor on plans for controlling farm production. They believed that attempts to support prices without any means of limiting output were doomed. One of the most widely discussed schemes for limiting farm output was the "domestic allotment plan," which had been proposed in an article in *Farm, Stock and Home*, published in Minneapolis. The article drew on ideas presented by W. J. Spillman, of the United States Department of Agriculture.* The plan was presented in detail by John D. Black of Harvard University in his book *Agricultural Reform in the United States*, published in 1929. The plan was taken up and promoted by several farm leaders and publicists, including Professor M. L. Wilson of Montana State College and Henry A. Wallace, editor of *Wallace's Farmer and Iowa Homestead*.

The domestic allotment plan would have established a domestic acreage allotment for each major crop on each farm.

* According to Murray R. Benedict, in the work cited in the last footnote.

It was believed that reducing acreage would reduce production enough to raise prices to a fair level for farmers. The domestic allotment plan was the basis for the original agricultural adjustment program put into effect by the New Deal in 1933 and 1934.

As an emergency relief measure the New Deal agricultural administration under Henry Wallace asked Congress for authority to make commodity loans on wheat, corn, cotton, and other crops. This was felt to be an incidental part of the main program, which was acreage adjustment. But the crop loans turned out to be the main show over the years. Acreage control never was very effective, except in the case of tobacco. And even in tobacco the results have been mixed.

Secretary Wallace also obtained authority for and carried out a sow and pig slaughter program in 1933 to reduce the supply of hogs on the fall and winter market. More political noise was made about this slaughter of sows and pigs than about any of the other New Deal farm actions. Critics belabored Wallace for "murdering" the little pigs (as though it were more heartless to slaughter a pig at 4 months of age than at 8 months).

The loans on corn, cotton, wheat, and tobacco were instantly successful and probably did more to make the New Deal in agriculture popular than anything else which was done. The commodity loans (price supports) have been the main feature of government farm programs ever since. Crop acreage allotments have continued down through the years— with the exception of the war and early postwar periods. But price supports have overshadowed controls as the main tool for protecting farm income.

The first commodity loans were not tied to any particular parity price level. Agriculture Secretary Wallace emphasized the goal of parity *income* for farmers. Neither the Department of Agriculture, farm-minded congressmen, nor farm leaders advocated parity prices—except as a vague target to shoot toward. Price supports in the thirties were not set at a fixed percentage of parity.

The Agricultural Adjustment Act of 1938, which was a sort of consolidation of experience under the early New Deal programs and was intended to establish a long-range formula for agricultural protection, set crop loans on a sliding scale between 52 and 75 per cent of parity. The loan rate for any year would be determined by the total supply in relation to expected consumption and exports. Even this moderate level of price support (by postwar standards) resulted in large accumulations of wheat and other basic crops (by pre-war standards).

But just about the time farmers and farm politicians be-gan to worry about how to handle the surpluses, World War II broke out. This cured the surplus ailment in a hurry and brought a demand for vastly greater output. Acreage controls were abandoned, and the government sought meth-ods of helping farmers grow more of nearly every crop and livestock product. One very effective method was a boost in price guarantees. Price support loans had been used to shield farmers from the effects of production outrunning demand. Now they were used as an incentive to raise more. Price guar-antees were first set at 85 per cent of parity, then within a few months lifted to 90 per cent. Not only the "basic" crops were included but also the "nonbasic" livestock and livestock products and a long list (forty-two commodities) of fruits, vegetables, and crops used as industrial raw materials.

Prices of most farm commodities quickly rose above the guaranteed levels under the influence of rising consumer demand, heavy government buying for the armed forces, and Lend-Lease. The Department of Agriculture had no worries about excess stocks in storage. Its worries were of another sort. It battled with the armed forces and manu-facturing industries for allocations of materials and other scarce resources for stepping up farm output. With the help of good weather, American agriculture achieved an enormous expansion in production and in basic productive capacity.*

This greatly expanded national farm "plant" remained in full operation after the war. It was needed to supply food for the hungry people of the war-devastated countries. Foreign relief aid and then Marshall Plan aid kept the total demand for American farm products roaring along at boom levels. Price guarantees stayed at 90 per cent of parity— extended by act of Congress a year or two at a time.

Trouble came first in potatoes and eggs.

In both cases production technology had advanced rapidly during the war years. DDT and fertilizer greatly lowered costs of potato production. New feeding and management practices, along with better disease control, had lowered egg production costs. The 90-per-cent-of-parity guarantee induced a heavy output—a bigger supply than consumers would buy at that price. As a result, the government had to buy large quantities to keep the price up to the legal guarantee.

By 1948 there were towering surpluses of potatoes in government storage above ground and thousands of tons of dried eggs in a government-owned salt mine in Kansas. The waste and diversion to lower uses of eggs and potatoes created a scandal. Some potatoes were doused in kerosene and burned, others dyed blue and fed to livestock. Dried eggs were used for livestock feed.

The potato and egg mess brought out a strong demand for flexible price guarantees. It resulted in the abandonment of price supports on these products. Neither the then secretary of agriculture, Charles F. Brannan, nor his successor, Ezra T. Benson, had the nerve to try to maintain guaranteed prices of eggs or potatoes after 1949.

* For a more complete discussion of the increase in farm production capacity during the war, see Walter W. Wilcox, *The Farmer in the Second World War*, Iowa State College Press, 1947.

However, Mr. Brannan went ahead with a buying program for dairy products, which are also quite perishable over a long period in storage. Surpluses of butter, cheese, and dried milk mounted, but Mr. Benson continued the 90 per cent support level the first year he was in office. After that he lowered the guarantees to 75 per cent of parity.

The Korean war temporarily took the pressure off. Foreign demand for grain and cotton increased, and prices soared above the price support levels. But by 1953, grain and cotton stocks were at an all-time high. And despite big cuts in acreage of wheat and cotton, production continued at about the same high level.

Wheat acreage was reduced by allotments from 62 million in 1954 to 55 million in 1955. But production advanced from 916 to 970 million bushels. Cotton farmers reduced plantings from 21 million acres in 1954 to 18 million in 1955, but the crop increased from 14 to 15 million bales.

Wheat farmers turned down compulsory marketing quotas in 1954 but voted in favor of them in 1955. These quotas place strict penalties on any farmer for selling wheat except that harvested on allotted acres, whether he voted in favor of quotas or not. Even this absolute control has relatively little effect on production. Farmers are able to increase yields on allotted acres by use of fertilizer and by better tillage enough to offset much of the reduction in acres.

This has been the history of crop acreage controls throughout the last twenty-two years. If the acreage cuts are large enough, of course, output will be reduced. But the reductions in acreage which have been politically possible have been mostly nullified by higher yields.

Acreage reductions have been least successful in the case of corn. Not only have they failed to reduce *corn* production, they have tended to *increase* production of other feeds which compete with corn. Diverted acres of all the "basic" crops usually are planted to alfalfa, clover, barley, oats, or other feed crops.

The cumulation of this effect has been to transfer part of the surplus of wheat and cotton to the feed-livestock sector of agriculture. By the end of 1955 the impact of the expansion in feed output was showing up in supplies of grain-fed cattle and hogs. Prices of meat animals sagged to the lowest levels in years—despite a high rate of consumer income and strong demand for meat.

After more than two decades of government efforts to protect farm product prices by means of acreage controls, crop loans, and purchases, the farmer was facing the same problem of excess production once again.

Roswell Garst, a farmer and hybrid seed corn producer, of Coon Rapids, Iowa, wrote a letter to an official in the Department of Agriculture in July 1955 about the propensity of farmers to increase output. This letter describes the rising productivity of agriculture and the surplus problem so well, that I am repeating the major part of it here, with Mr. Garst's permission:

"In 1949 we were producing a million tons of actual nitrogen for agricultural use in the United States. The Korean War, which started in 1950 and ran through 1951, caused such a demand for food, both domestically and abroad, that food became scarce and high priced and started off a rather violent inflation because of the spiralling prices of food during this period. We were not actually producing enough food in 1951 to feed ourselves amply at a fair price and export what friendly nations demanded. Forty dollar cattle and corn at $1.80 or above were pretty fair indicators of the situation. Furthermore, the likelihood of World War III breaking out was great, as is clearly proven by the very great enlargement of our defense appropriations.

"Secretary Brannan, realizing that the fastest way to produce more food was to produce more nitrogen, called my brother, Jonathan Garst, down to Washington and put him in charge of securing an expansion of the nitrogen fixation facilities so that we could produce more food, and Certificates of Necessity were issued and steel allotted and a tax amortization speed-up allowed so that nitrogen fixation could be increased by a million tons.

"That is one reason I am particularly familiar with the situation. That first million tons of nitrogen production should be listed as a defense measure, right along with the armaments. By January 1, 1954 the U.S. had 2 million tons of nitrogen available for agricultural purposes. But, having gotten the habit of building plants, the chemical industry has continued, and the administration with which you are connected, has, I believe, continued to encourage nitrogen fixation plants to the extent that the fertilizer section says that by January 1, 1957, the U.S. will be producing 4 million tons of nitrogen for agricultural purposes. I believe the production is currently running at the rate of about 3 million tons of nitrogen for agricultural purposes—that is, up roughly a million tons this year over last year.

"Two pounds of nitrogen, when properly used, in combination with phosphorus, potash, calcium, and other good farming practices, is equivalent to one bushel of corn. If you apply 50 pounds of nitrogen per acre to 40 acres of land you will have used one ton of nitrogen and you will have increased corn yields 25 bushels per acre on 40 acres and will have produced 1,000 more bushels of corn. That makes it an easy figure. If we use a million tons of nitrogen intelligently on our corn and in combination with other fertilizers and other good farm practices, we will produce a *billion* extra bushels of corn.

"Nor is corn the only crop, by any means, where it works— it works on oats, wheat, barley, grain sorghums—and it works best of all on grass pastures. Both the University of Missouri and Wisconsin—I guess you might include practically every experiment station in the U.S.—have clearly proved that well fertilized pastures will produce two or three times as much beef, mutton or milk, as unfertilized pastures —I think they will tell you that the increases from grass are normally higher percentagewise than from grain.

"Furthermore, the fertilizer section of the Department of Agriculture will tell you that the production of phosphorus and potash has expanded so that the nitrogen can be intelligently used—and that the increase in crop production on a per acre basis is exploding. The little fire that is now burning in the basement of the house of agriculture is gaining momentum.

"Nitrogen means proteins. We have always had ample carbohydrates, and never enough protein for best feeding efficiency. Now comes urea—this is another small example. When I first started using urea in 1948 it was practically unknown. Only DuPont made it in the U.S. and for feeding purposes, only experimentally. Research proved very definitely that up to one-third of the total protein intake, urea is as good a form of protein as are by-product meals. The cost of a pound of protein in the form of urea is approximately 2 cents. The cost of a pound of protein in the form of by-product meal has averaged more than 8 cents in the last 10 year period. So it was only natural that the use of urea would expand. From no urea in 1948 the use of urea grew to where in the current year we are using more than 70,000 tons of urea in mixed cattle feeds. That replaces 425,000 tons of soybean or cottonseed meal. It would take something like 15 million bushels of beans to make that much soybean meal. Nor are we through increasing. Where only DuPont made a little experimentally in 1948, now you have DuPont, Allied Chemical, the Grace Chemical Company, the John Deere Plow Company, all producing it in big quantities that I know of—and there are probably more.

"I suspect that the use of urea in mixed feeds will double

in the next three year period. We are going to have twice as much urea as we feed now—substituting for twice as much soybean meal—or probably more likely, adding to the supply of proteins so that more livestock is better fed than ever before.

"As little as five years ago, it took about three and a half pounds of feed to make one pound of broiler meat. This was the average for the U.S. Now if you cannot produce a pound of broiler meat with three pounds of feed you cannot stay in business—I think actually it is getting down now to where successful broiler people figure on a pound of broiler meat for every 2.8 or 2.9 pounds of feed. That's a 20 per cent increase in feed efficiency in a five year period, or thereabouts, largely due to antibiotics. Stilbestrol is now being fed to approximately all the cattle on feed in the U.S. and the U.S.D.A. figures show that it steps up the efficiency of cattle feeding by 11 per cent.

"You have to live out here to see what is happening—and know for sure and without question what is going to happen. What has happened up to date is phenomenal—what will happen is even more phenomenal—and we simply cannot go on in agriculture with either a 90 per cent of parity program, or a fluctuating program, that is based upon facts as they existed 20 years ago—or, five years ago.

"If you cut the acreage in Iowa 20 per cent in corn, 90 per cent of the farmers can increase their corn yield more than 20 per cent by just putting on more fertilizer, better balanced fertilizer—Aldrin for rootworms—corn borer spray in quantity and properly applied—and then they can raise pretty nearly as much beef and milk per acre on the grass that they seed in increased quantities as they would with the present corn crop. If you have cross-compliance* for a four

* This means that land taken out of production of one crop, say corn, by an allotment program cannot be planted to another controlled crop, say wheat, and must go to grass.

year period, we won't think of 95 million head of cattle as being large numbers—125 million head will be modest.

"Nor is this increase in productivity to be deplored. We used to use 100 million acres of corn to produce 2.6 million bushels, back in the Twenties. Now we use 80 million acres to produce 3.2 billion bushels of corn—shortly we will be using 70 million acres to produce 3.5 billion bushels of corn. We are a well-fed nation, protein-wise, but we could be a better fed nation, protein-wise—and we will be a better fed nation. We have exported a good deal of agricultural products in the past—we can and should export much more in the future. I don't think any one thing can possibly solve the problem—I think we are going to have to use every tool and every bit of imagination we possess to solve the problem—and not break farmers in the process."

Perhaps this is a bit overstated. But its essential point is one which careful analysis by America's best-qualified agricultural economists bears out. Sherman Johnson, of the Agricultural Research Service of the United States Department of Agriculture, who probably has devoted more time to study of farm production and farm productivity trends than any other person in an official position, agrees in general with Garst's implied projections. That is, he believes the agricultural production revolution is still gathering momentum. A study by James T. Bonnen of Michigan State University and John D. Black of Harvard University, for the National Planning Association, indicates that food production will continue to rise faster than population to 1965. Projections made by Dr. Black for the president's Materials Policy Commission (Paley Commission) point to the probability of supply of farm products outdistancing demand for these products to 1975 at least.

Bonnen and Black conclude that "The annual surplus of production is likely to become more severe, continuous and

CHART 9. U.S. Population and Farm Output

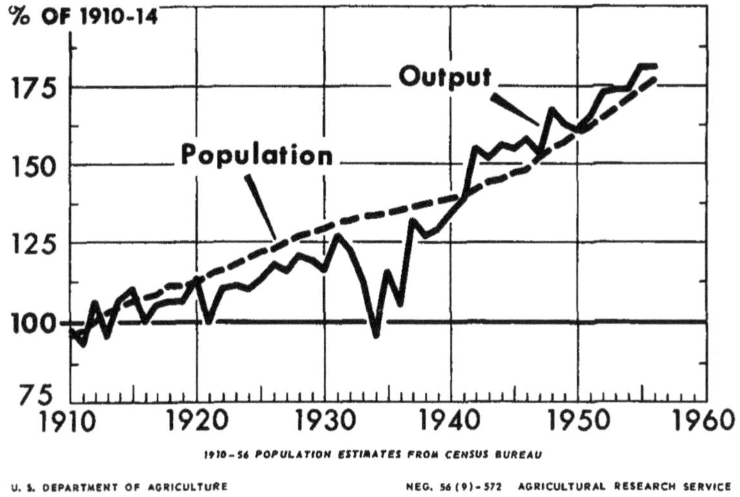

% OF 1910-14

175

150

125

100

75

1910   1920   1930   1940   1950   1960

1910-56 POPULATION ESTIMATES FROM CENSUS BUREAU

U. S. DEPARTMENT OF AGRICULTURE   NEG. 56 (9)-572   AGRICULTURAL RESEARCH SERVICE

apparently permanent if no more effective measures are taken than at present. . . .

"In every major commodity group yields will increase more than production needs by 1965. . . . We are obviously not going to 'eat our way out' through increases in per capita consumption and in population; the total effect of both of these factors is to lift food consumption no more than 20 per cent. While yields are expected to increase by only 23 per cent, the maximum yield increase possible by 1965 for food products combined ranges up over 60 per cent. . . . With no production controls and present prices a 30 per cent increase in food production by 1965 is well within the bounds of possibility."

In brief, the supply of farm products is growing faster than the demand for these products and gives every indication of continuing to do so.

Demand for farm products as a group is much less elastic than demand for nonfarm products and services. As the economy becomes richer and the standard of living rises this relative inelasticity of demand for farm products (mainly food) tends to become more striking. People continue to demand about the same quantity of food regardless of price changes. Or, to put it the other way around, a larger supply sends prices tumbling sharply, because consumers will not spend more money to get more than their accustomed quantities.

In poor countries, where people live close to the nutritional margin, a moderate reduction in prices can bring about a considerable increase in consumption. But not in the United States.

Demand for the higher-priced "luxury" foods is growing more inelastic in the United States. Even in Adam Smith's day, demand for wheat was noticeably less flexible than demand for manufactured products. Today in this country the consumer reacts to changes in prices of meat, milk, eggs, fruits, and such higher-quality foods as his great grandfather reacted to changes in prices of bread. That is, we consider these "luxury" foods necessities.

The consequence of this change in demand is that prices of such products are more sensitive to changes in supply than they were before. Farmers have to take less money for a large supply of hogs than for a small supply. The price per unit drops more than enough to offset the increased volume. Even as recently as twenty-five or thirty years ago, demand for meat appeared to be relatively elastic. Dr. Geoffrey Shepherd of Iowa State College concluded in the mid-thirties, using data for the preceding ten or fifteen years, that demand for hogs was "unilastic": a large supply would sell for about the same number of dollars as a small supply; the price per unit would change about in inverse proportion to the change in supply. Today consumers do not respond as strongly to meat price reductions or raises.

The gradual change in the character of the demand for food in our rich economy as it grows still richer is of profound importance to farmers. Until very recently it could be assumed that an adjustment of farm production from grains and potatoes to livestock, fruits, and leafy vegetables would "cure" the farm surplus problem. Now we cannot be so sure this will do it.

Such a shift in production is going on, will continue to go on, and *should* go on, because that is what consumer choice is directing. It will help ease the surplus problem, because the same amounts of land, labor, and capital will produce fewer calories of food in these products than in wheat and potatoes. The adjustment to a higher-quality product in agriculture, however, will not eliminate the income instability problem which is associated with erratic supply. In a sense, we are now engaged in transferring the farm surplus from wheat, cotton (which also has suffered from inelasticity of demand) potatoes, and other cash crops to livestock, fruit, and vegetables.

The faster this adjustment can proceed, the easier will be the over-all surplus problem. But it will not be eliminated in the visible future.

9

Too Many Farmers

What can be done to reduce the pressure of excess supplies on prices of farm products—to balance demand and supply at a level which will give farmers incomes on a parity with nonfarm incomes?

One answer, of course, is to do nothing, let "nature" take her course. This answer appeals to many who have a philosophical distaste for government intervention into private business. But it has no chance of being adopted as a national policy. The belief that farmers are entitled to incomes equal to those earned in other occupations demanding the same ability and effort is a part of twentieth century mores. Both major political parties favor government action to redress the balance between agriculture and the rest of the population.

A "do nothing" policy would be feasible if the community were willing to see the basic agricultural adjustment between demand and supply take place by means of bankruptcy, liquidation, and abandonment of farms. This process of attrition would mean that the best brains, the most capable young people would leave farming even faster than they now are leaving. It might mean that fifty or so years hence agriculture would fall far behind the rest of the economy in technical efficiency. Meanwhile, with a growing population, it is possible that real food shortages would overtake us.

Americans need only look to the outside world to see what an inefficient agriculture can do to an economy. High productivity per man in farming is a priceless asset that permits America to devote relatively little manpower to supplying basic food and fiber needs. A sharp contrast may be seen in the

Soviet Union, which I visited in the summer of 1955 as a member of the American farm delegation. The Soviets have neglected agriculture until recently, putting their major emphasis on industrialization. Farm living standards have been kept low by deliberate policy of the state. The state has used farming as a source of capital for manufacturing development. The result has been a stagnation in agricultural production. The U.S.S.R. even now has 40 to 45 per cent of its people in agriculture. It has no surpluses; it runs on the borderline of hunger all the time. Diets are not as rich in protein foods as they were before World War I.

The Soviet high command belatedly has come to a realization that agricultural efficiency must be fostered and promoted if food production is not to be a drag on the entire economy. But the task is overwhelming because of the late start.

In contrast, look at the United States. For more than 100 years our basic agricultural policy has been to stimulate agricultural production and to encourage technological advance. The preservation of the Union so dominates our thinking about the administration of Abraham Lincoln that we may forget its importance in charting the economic future of the nation. It was in 1862 that two fundamental policies were laid down which have been the backbone of our economic development. These were expressed in the Homestead Act, which stimulated the private development of land resources, and the Morrill Act, which set the stage for the land grant college system of agricultural experiment stations and Extension Services.

Here was direct government action, subsidy if you please, for stepping up the farm production of the country. The free land was practically all taken up by the end of the century, although some homesteading has gone on in the twentieth. And it was about at the turn of the century that the agricultural research and educational program began to take hold.

Thus in the last half of the nineteenth century we had a great, subsidized injection of land resources into the farm economy. In the first half of this century we have had an even more powerful injection of new, scientific technology into agriculture.

In the light of this historical background, it should not be surprising that supply of and demand for farm products have got out of balance in the last thirty-five years. If there were no other reason for community responsibility to the farm population, the fact that public policies created the present surplus situation would be reason enough. The "built-in" tendency for farm production to expand faster than demand for food is a consequence not only of the century-old public subsidy for technological improvement, but also of the enormous stimulation to production during the last fifteen years by wartime and postwar public policy.

Letting nature take its course has not been American farm policy for 100 years; to adopt it now would be to ask 22 million farm people to bear the burden of adjustment for which the whole community is responsible.

Understanding the causes of the surplus situation in farming leads to some logical solutions. Why not a homestead policy in reverse, for example? Theodore W. Schultz of the University of Chicago has suggested that the federal government offer farm families a cash payment to help them get started in city life and nonfarm work. Such a payment, say $5,000, would be given only for bona fide transfers out of agriculture. That is, families would have to meet the same kinds of tests of sincerity of their determination to carve out a new life as the homesteaders had to meet. Administration of such a program would be difficult. Safeguards would be needed to prevent families from moving off a farm to collect the cash subsidy and then moving back to another farm.

But ignoring administrative difficulties (which our resourceful lawyers undoubtedly could find ways to overcome), the plan is entirely logical. The government subsidized people *into* agriculture in the last century—and still does through credit assistance, the veterans farm education program, and other ways—so why not subsidize people who want to move *out* of farming?

Speeding up the movement of some farmers out of agriculture would permit those who remain to increase the size of their operations and raise their incomes. The national farm income would be divided among fewer people. The movement of farmers into other occupations would also tend to reduce farm production and thus ease the surplus problem. Transferring cityward people who produce little for market would not reduce total production. But Schultz suggests applying the "homesteads-in-reverse" idea to commercial farmers. He would provide such a subsidy to a family which had produced at least $2,500 worth of farm products in the preceding year. Transfer of such farm families to city work would tend to cut farm production.*

Encouraging people to move out of farming if they have a chance to improve their incomes by so doing would help the surplus situation in another way. It would tend to increase the commercial demand for food, because city families do not produce as much of their own food as do farm families.

If such a homesteads-in-reverse program were in effect, it would prevent a great deal of hardship. Farm folks would not stay on the farm until they had lost everything. Those with little liking for and ability in agriculture would get a chance to better themselves. Many such families now are tied down to farms they cannot afford to leave. If they could be helped into nonfarm work, many of them would make a much greater contribution to national production.

I have known of a number of farm families gradually forced out of farming around Des Moines who could have

---

* All good farm land would still be farmed, but much of it less intensively than before with less labor available.

been spared years of hardship by governmental assistance. One was a college graduate who now makes four times as much income in a factory job as he made farming. This sort of lubrication of the free market in employment seems wholly appropriate to the American governmental system. It certainly is not a new concept in our society.

"Natural" economic forces are just too slow and too cruel and too inefficient to meet the needs of our growing economy for this sort of an adjustment. Subsidies for the transfer of people out of agriculture would be subsidies to farm people that would be corrective of a basic maladjustment. Too many of the subsidies of the last twenty-five years have been such as to hold people on farms. The "homesteads-in-reverse" idea is unique in that it would raise incomes of people now living on farms without freezing them to the farms. In fact, it would put a premium on leaving agriculture.

This will not appeal to those agricultural fundamentalists who want to keep the farm population from dwindling. It will not appeal to those farm leaders who think every farmer should be guaranteed an income regardless of his efficiency. Nor will it appeal to the most emotional of the "small family farm" advocates. Obviously, this program of subsidizing people out of agriculture would tend to increase the size of farms. In some areas it might mean very large-scale, "corporate" farms. But, judging by the results of movement away from farms in the first half of this century, the primary effect would be larger *family* farms—not a wholesale conversion of the individual enterpriser system of farming to "factory" farms.

It cannot be emphasized too much that the fundamental adjustment needed to take care of the surplus situation in American agriculture is a reduction in the number of farm families. The question is whether this adjustment should be allowed to take place "by itself," without help from the state, or should be smoothed and speeded up by a subsidy.

Many of our public policies and programs in agriculture conflict directly with the policy of reducing surpluses. In fact, practically all government intervention in agriculture is on the side of *increasing* output—with the exception of the acreage allotment programs, and they have not been effective in limiting output.

The influences of price supports and soil conservation programs are discussed in later chapters. I have shown in Chapter 7 how public research and education stimulate greater and greater production of farm products. Tax concessions and other incentives have contributed to increased supplies of commercial fertilizer. Many other instances of federal and state action which intensify the surplus problem could be cited.

Wherever possible, public policies should be changed to reduce this pressure toward greater output. It is senseless to continue policies working against each other.

Almost the entire federal and state bureaucracy in agriculture is mobilized to get farmers to produce more—at the same time that acreage allotments and the "soil bank" are being tightened down to limit production. Agricultural officialdom and the major farm organizations are alike in their inconsistency on this point. The Farm Bureau, the Grange, and the Farmers Union all are in favor of increased appropriations for farm research—most of which is in production technology and is therefore output-increasing. Secretary Benson asks for bigger funds for research in farm production at the same time he asks for a soil bank program to cut output. He complains that the high price supports passed by Congress provide incentives which work against the acreage limitation programs. But he seems not to see that new technology has the same effect.

What agriculture needs is more research in economics and the other social sciences to provide answers to the complex human adjustments required. But we continue to steer the bulk of our research and educational personnel and facilities into stepping up the output of commercial agriculture.

Of course it is true that advances in science are beneficial to society as a whole, and one should not take a short-run view of these matters. There are strong reasons, compelling reasons, for continuing or even increasing funds for research in basic science. What is questionable policy, however, is the pumping of more money into the development of *new technology* from this basic research right now.

New technology can be considered as a resource of production, like land, machinery, or fertilizer. Why not slow down expansion in this field in the same way that we hold land out of use until it is needed? Since research funds are limited, why not allocate more of them to projects which will help reduce surpluses rather than increase them?

I realize that this suggestion will sound like heresy to the professional agricultural fraternity—and to many farmers. Our whole tradition is in a contrary direction. Some readers will say I am against progress in scientific agriculture. I am not, as I think I have made clear in earlier chapters. All I suggest is that some *shift in emphasis* in agricultural research would help slow down the drive to greater production—and would be consistent with the major national programs to balance supply with demand. Let us stockpile knowledge in fundamental science for use in farm technology as we can absorb it. This is done by other industries; corporations deliberately plan the introduction of new technology. Why not agriculture?

The rebuttal to this suggestion is easy to make. Improved technology increases output *per man* and has nothing to do with total output or the balance of supply and demand. True. If we could adjust the number of people in farming rapidly enough to absorb the new technology, there would be no problems of surpluses or low farm income. But, as a practical matter, the push for efficiency increases *total* output and reduces farm income per person. Inelastic demand for farm products results in less return to agriculture for larger supplies.

I repeat that the *major* solution to the surplus situation is to help people to get out of farming. Meanwhile, it might be a good idea to spend more for research and education directed to *that* solution and less on new production technology.

10

Price Supports

American agricultural policy since World War I has relied heavily on government pricing as a means of meeting the overproduction (and low price) problem. Farmers and their organizations usually have put their political emphasis on raising prices. They have noted that their costs often remain the same or advance while prices of their products sag. In the twenties they looked back to a period of favorable terms of trade just before World War I, and this became "parity," the sacred goal of farm policy.

The farm plans of the twenties, as noted in Chapter 8, were nearly all schemes to push prices of farm products higher—by manipulations in the export market, by controlling production and marketing, or by outright price-fixing. Experiments in the thirties with crop acreage controls, export dumping, and various other programs were only partially successful. In the Agricultural Adjustment Act of 1938, Washington finally turned to government guarantees of prices. These were limited guarantees, ranging only from 52 to 75 per cent of parity for basic crops depending on the supplies. Then during World War II, primarily as a means of stimulating production, Congress adopted a system of much higher price guarantees, covering practically all the important farm products. Farmers were promised 90 per cent of parity for all they could grow.

Price supports continued to be the main tool of government action in agriculture after the war. The 90 per cent guarantees remained in effect for basic crops until the end of 1954. So the nation has had a good deal of experience with government price fixing in agriculture. How well has it worked?

One conclusion may be surely drawn: price supports have not been an effective method of dealing with the long-run tendency of farm production to grow faster than demand. They have not helped correct the surplus situation. They have made it worse, by providing incentives to farmers to increase rather than decrease production.

Price supports have increased incomes of wheat, rice, cotton, tobacco, peanut, and cash corn producers. But they have done so only at the cost of worsening the basic supply situation or making it harder to deal with. It was necessary to reduce drastically the acreage allotments of both wheat and cotton when government stocks rose after the Korean war. These cuts in acreage were only partly effective in reducing output, despite the use of compulsory marketing quotas which prevented the sale of crops except from the allotted acres. Farmers voted to restrict themselves by these quotas in return for higher price supports, but they partially nullified the effect of this by exerting themselves zealously to increase yields per acre.

High price guarantees not only stimulate output. They also limit markets. In three years from June 1952 to June 1955, the Commodity Credit Corporation accumulated more than 5½ billion dollars' worth of commodities which could not be sold at the supported price.

It is quite evident that the price support tool has been misused repeatedly during the postwar years. Farm leaders and politicians have looked upon the price of a commodity only as the yardstick of immediate economic well-being for the producers of the commodity. But in addition to determining the return a farmer gets for a given volume of production, the price also serves as a regulator of consumption and a guide to production. A price kept far out of line with demand and supply may give farmers income protection for a while. But if it does not perform its other functions of guiding production and consumption properly, farmers will be the losers in the end. High price guarantees are self-defeating in the long run.

The unhappy results in the early fifties from price supports for some commodities that were far too high should not blind us to the useful function price supports can serve—in helping to stabilize prices. Many of the swings of prices of farm products are much more violent than necessary to induce proper use of resources. Agriculture's free markets, so gloriously extolled in some quarters, often have worked rather poorly in guiding output. Those who fulminate at government price fixing as undiluted evil need to face up to some of the evils of the free market. The huge gyrations in hog prices in the 1952-56 period are an excellent example. Demand for pork and lard was stable at a high level during this period. Yet production of hogs varied greatly, with consequent large changes in hog prices. In the summer of 1954, hog prices were around $25 per hundredweight; in the winter of 1955 many farmers sold hogs for as low as $10.

Such catastrophic declines in hog prices serve no useful purpose. There probably is a loss in efficiency from farmers' going into and out of hog production. Both consumers and producers would be better served by a more stable price pattern.

The same sort of extreme cyclical behavior of production and prices occurs in the cases of grain-fed cattle, eggs, poultry, meat, vegetable crops, and some fruits. Total beef production moves up and down in a longer cycle, often as long as sixteen years. Cycles in production of tree fruits, such as apples and oranges, are also long-term.

Free-market prices plainly give incorrect signals to producers on many occasions, just as government price supports at too high a level give incorrect signals. What is needed is government action that will moderate the short-time ups and downs in prices of farm products without interfering with the

long-run trends of prices caused by changes in demand and
the costs of production.

The failures of price supports in recent years are attrib-
utable to two reasons: first, dependence upon a formula,
"parity," to establish the level of support, and, second, the
attempt to accomplish both stability and income support by
means of price guarantees.

In the American governmental system the executive is
given relatively little freedom in economic matters. Congress
usually ties down the administrators by means of specific
formulae and limits on their discretionary authority. Thus
the parity formula and the stated limits of price supports
have prevented secretaries of agriculture from adjusting
prices even when the needed adjustment was plain for all
to see. For example, Secretary Brannan was compelled by
law to keep on buying eggs and potatoes at 90 per cent of
parity while stocks deteriorated in storage. It must be said,
however, that most secretaries of agriculture have preferred
to be tied down by specific laws, rather than face the political
pressure when the decision was left up to them.

The British are more sophisticated about these things.
Farm price guarantees are set by the government, without
regard to any formula, in consultation with farm organizations. This actually is a form of collective bargaining on farm
prices, similar to wage bargaining by labor unions. Eventually, the United States may have to come to such a system.
The Committee for Economic Development recommended
in January 1956 that an agricultural stabilization board be
established with authority to determine price support levels.

If price support operations by the government are to be
most useful in serving the function of stabilization, then
either a nonpartisan public board such as the CED recom-
mends or the secretary of agriculture himself must be given
power to set levels of support without regard to any rigid
formula. Since the secretary of agriculture is a political officer,

subject to all the forces of party politics, it would seem wiser to turn this job over to a board insulated as much as possible from such influences. A board with status similar to that of the Federal Reserve Board certainly could serve the public interest better than a parity formula which inevitably lags behind economic changes.

But the main reform needed in price supports is to establish the principle that price guarantees are for the purpose of stabilization—not for the purpose of raising farm incomes or affecting the long-run trends of prices. No administrator can perform the function of adjusting price relationships over time as well as the free market reflecting consumer choices, changing export demands, and the costs of production. Price support operations by the government should be conceived as a *supplement* to the free market, a means of moderating extreme changes. The public purpose of achieving greater equality in incomes should be left to other methods.

11

Helping the Market Work Better

If the federal government is to be most effective in moderating the extreme swings in prices of farm products, and thus helping the free market guide production more rationally, then administrative officials should have considerable leeway in setting price support levels. They should not be bound by a rigid formula such as parity, even though on a "sliding scale." Administrative officials also should have the authority to use a variety of methods of price stabilization.

Generally speaking, Congress has insisted that the Department of Agriculture support prices of farm products by actually buying the products, or by making nonrecourse loans to farmers on commodities, which is practically the same as buying them. This method of price support works well enough for products which can be easily stored for long periods, such as cotton and wheat. It does not work so well for perishable products such as meat and dairy products.

In the winter of 1943-44 the Department of Agriculture was faced with a difficult task in trying to make good on the government guarantee of hog prices at 90 per cent of parity. An enormous pig crop in 1943 flooded the winter markets and sent prices below the guarantee. The Department tried to buy enough pork to hold the market up to 90 per cent of parity but was unsuccessful. Secretaries of agriculture have been leery of price guarantees on livestock ever since.

The experience with price supports on eggs, potatoes, and dairy products after World War II also was unfavorable. In these cases the government was able to make good on the price guarantees but only by building up great supplies of perishable products in storage. Some spoilage occurred, and part of the stocks had to be sold for lower uses—potatoes for alcohol and dried eggs and milk for livestock feed. These costs were not excessive in relation to the total gain to farmers. But they were "open game" for political criticism of price supports. The egg and potato "mess" was so widely denounced that Congress abandoned any guarantees for these commodities. No matter how large the surpluses, no matter how well fed the American public, waste of food is very bad politics.

Because of these experiences (and others) in supporting prices of perishable products by purchases, a number of proposals have been made to provide producers of such commodities outright cash payments instead of price support. The idea is to pay farmers the difference between the government guarantee and the actual market price in cash. For example, suppose hog prices were guaranteed at $18 per hundred pounds and the market price sank to $14. Then hog producers would get a payment of $4 per hundred from the government.

This plan has been recommended on various occasions by a large proportion of the members of the Farm Economic Association, by congressmen of both the Democratic and Republican parties, by at least two secretaries of agriculture, by the National Farmers Union and at one time by the Iowa Farm Bureau Federation (but never the national organization of the Farm Bureau), and by assorted other agricultural opinion makers. The authority to use this method of protecting farmers' returns from perishable farm products was included in the first postwar agricultural act, the Hope-Aiken Act of 1948. This authority was removed in the 1949 revision of the law. The provision for methods of price support was so ambiguous that neither Secretary Brannan nor Secretary Benson was willing to take the chance of making direct price payments.

Under the Sugar Act, however, direct payments are made to producers, and the 1954 farm act provides for compensatory payments to wool producers in lieu of market price support. Secretary Benson, one of the stanchest opponents of the direct payment principle, approved of this method for sugar and wool.

Payments of this general nature have long been used in other countries, notably the United Kingdom.

In spite of all this record of backing for a payment system to stabilize returns to producers of livestock and other perishable commodities, it has not become politically feasible in peacetime in the United States—except for relatively minor commodities such as sugar and wool.

As Walter Lippmann has pointed out, Americans generally prefer their subsidies in indirect form. Partly this is a matter of self-deception to make intervention by the state in economic affairs seem to be something else. For example, the protective tariff has been acceptable even to rigidly doctrinaire "free enterprisers" who deplore "socialistic intervention" in private business. Of course the effects of a tariff are the same as a direct subsidy in helping producers meet the rigors of competition. But the hand of the government is not out in the open, and no government spending is involved. So the tariff is considered part of "the free enterprise system."

In agriculture this typically American reluctance to take "handouts" from the government has been an especially big factor in policy. Farm Bureau leaders talk piously about farmers getting their returns "in the market place" instead of from government. Yet they do not exclude government price supports from their concept of "in the market place." They argue that if farm price guarantees were made good by direct payments, farmers would be dependent on annual appropriations by Congress.

Commodity loans and purchases to support prices also depend on government appropriations. However, the view of farm leaders is that a guaranteed price can be maintained by production controls and storage with a minimum administrative expense. Thus what the public sees in government outlays is smaller than would be the case with direct payments. Like a tariff, market price supports can remain relatively invisible—in theory.

Why should farm groups be politically sensitive on this point? Farm people have political power far beyond their numbers both in state legislatures and in the national government. This is because changes in legislative districts lag far behind changes in population—also because the United States Senate gives low-population rural states as much voting power in that body as metropolitan states. Still, farm leaders are conscious of the rapid decline in farm population and can foresee the gradual reduction of farm political power. This may be the intuitive reason why the big farm organizations except the Farmers Union have opposed direct payments to farmers. They do not want agriculture's government aid in such plainly visible form, because they fear they will be outvoted by consumers.

This is not a completely consistent position. The farm organizations have not objected to payments for soil conservation practices. But conservation payments can be more easily justified as in the whole national interest than price payments.

From a practical economic standpoint the direct payment method has many advantages, especially and obviously in the case of perishable products. How much more sensible to let the market price sink to whatever level will move all the meat, milk, eggs, potatoes into consumption—and then pay farmers in cash whatever subsidy is deemed necessary! Even in the case of durable products, such as wheat and cotton, once a safe national reserve is in storage, why not let the market price serve its function of adjusting supply and demand—giving producers a direct payment instead of a loan for putting more in storage?

No uniform method of guaranteeing prices of farm products will be suitable for all products—nor for any one product at all times. For sugar producers, a relatively small group, checks from the United States Treasury may be an efficient method. For livestock producers, numbering in the millions, it probably would be administratively simpler to pay the subsidies through the packing industry. This was done during the war to give livestock producers higher returns than would have been possible otherwise under the meat price ceilings. The government paid the money to packers, who passed it on to farmers with their ordinary payments for livestock purchased. The same technique works well with the dairy industry.

In *total* cost to the American public such payments to farmers probably would be less than the equivalent subsidy through government buying and storage. Consumers would get their meat and milk at lower prices, which would be an offset against the greater outlay by government.

Farm leaders often say that direct payments are really a subsidy to consumers and represent a "cheap food philosophy." There is truth in this. Prices of food would be lower to consumers under a direct payment system. But is this bad? Is it not sounder policy to let people eat all the food produced rather than to put it in warehouses in order to keep market prices high? Though farm leaders fear a visible subsidy and "dependence on appropriations," city people might respond favorably to a farm program which emphasized consumption. You can hardly expect consumers to be enthusiastic about a price support program which holds products off the market.

Lobbyists for farm organizations often say that farmers do not want cash handouts from the government. But there is little convincing evidence that this is so. Farmers have willingly accepted checks from the government for soil conservation for many years. Opinion surveys have indicated that most farmers would have no objection to payments on price guarantees. Farmers are more realistic than the politicians on this point, perhaps, and less sensitive to the differences between visible and invisible subsidies.

Direct payments to producers, if based on too high a level of price guarantees, would encourage a continuing expansion in production beyond the needs of consumers. Payments quickly would mount to exorbitant sums. This would lead either to drastic limitations on production, with quotas to farmers, or to abandonment of the whole support plan.

The danger in setting price supports too high is a danger not confined to the direct payment method. This has been demonstrated clearly in the cotton and wheat price support programs. To avoid such mistakes in pricing, the concept of the function of price supports must be changed. Instead of using price guarantees as a means of raising farm income, we should use them primarily as a means of stabilizing market prices and of helping the market do a better job of steering production into the right things and the right amounts. This is enough of a task for price supports, without getting into the problem of equalizing farm incomes with nonfarm incomes.

If price supports were to be used in this way, the guarantee would be set safely below the average market price to be expected during a production cycle.* The aim would be

---

* Of course, the nearer the guarantee could come to the average market price, the better the job of price stabilization. Such a guarantee also would be better from the viewpoint of guiding production. There is a vast reservoir of experience in price-prediction in the Department of Agriculture, through the Farm Outlook work, which would be helpful in setting price-stabilizing guarantees. Actual experience would be the best teacher, however, and the degree of success attainable would vary by commodities. For some commodities it might be feasible simply to extend a short-time market price average, or a percentage of it. If the price of commodity X averaged $1 per unit for the preceding year, the government could announce a guarantee of 90 cents for the next year. As market prices changed in a major movement upward or downward, the guarantee would lag behind

to even out the excessive swings in market prices, not to change the long-run trend of prices. Consumer tastes, changes in production costs, and changes in export demand would determine the relationships among prices of different commodities. These factors, therefore, would chart the direction of change in American agricultural production. Government "price fixers" would not usurp the role of the market in steering the use of farm resources.

But government price guarantees would serve to check extreme short-run changes in prices. Let us see how they might work in stabilizing hog prices and production.

In response to rising prices of hogs in the Korean war of 1950 and 1951, farmers raised a huge crop of pigs in 1951. When these pigs were marketed, prices fell sharply. This caused a reduction in pig production in 1952 and 1953, so prices rose in 1954. In the winter of 1952-53, hog prices at Chicago averaged around $17 a hundred pounds. A year later they were around $25. The $25 hogs in the winter of 1953-54, and higher prices throughout 1954, induced farmers to raise more pigs in 1955. Down went prices again in the last half of 1955 and in 1956. Since cattle marketings were also increasing in 1955, prices of hogs hit new lows for the postwar years—down to around $11 and even less at times in December and January.

These huge variations in hog prices—from over $20 to $10 within one year—were a consequence of unstable production. Consumer demand for pork was steady at a high level during all these years. Hog production is closely related to the supply and price of corn. But in the years 1951 to 1955, corn was a stabilizing rather than an unstabilizing influence on hog production. Prices were supported at 90 per cent of parity by the government loans, and supplies were

---

but would have a stabilizing effect—and would help prevent huge changes in farmers' production plans. The techniques of forward price guarantees would necessarily be different for different products.

adequate. In fact, corn reserves increased each year of this period. So the gyrations in hog production must have been caused almost entirely by farmers guessing wrong on prices. They overshot the market on supplies in 1951, again in 1955, and undershot in the intervening years.

In this kind of a situation, sensible government price policy could do much to even out the flow of supplies and the movements of prices. A hog price guarantee of around $18 or $19 announced in 1952 for the year 1953 probably would have prevented such a sharp drop in pig production in 1952. With a "stop loss" guarantee, farmers would have been more likely to maintain their usual production. Prices in 1952-53 would not have risen to $25 and higher. The terrific incentive to expand pig production in 1954 and 1955 would not have been quite so terrific. And prices might not have fallen to such depths in 1955-56.

The same technique of forward price guarantees could be used to help smooth the price swings of many farm commodities. To get the best results, the authority for adjusting these guarantees, within wide limits, should be lodged in an independent price stabilization board, with a status something like that of the Federal Reserve Board in monetary policy. Price setting by formula and by Congressional action would have to be thrown overboard. It would take a maturity and sophistication of political behavior which unhappily has not been demonstrated in the field of farm legislation to date.

Price stabilization problems are different for each farm commodity. They can be dealt with intelligently by government only when responsible officials have wide authority both as to methods and as to price levels. For some commodities, price "targets" or guarantees would need to be changed frequently. For others, only once in several years, perhaps. Any general pattern of price support which treats cotton, wheat, corn, peanuts, hogs, milk, and potatoes in the same way cannot work satisfactorily.

12

Ever-Normal Granary

The severe droughts of 1934 and 1936 took the minds of Corn Belt and Great Plains farmers off the surplus problem temporarily. They became concerned about livestock feed shortages. Large numbers of livestock had to be liquidated during these years because of insufficient feed. The annual wheat harvests in the 1933-36 period averaged about a third less than in the preceding ten years. No shortage of wheat for domestic consumption occurred, but prices rose sharply and exports were greatly reduced. There was much talk in farm groups about the need for efforts to stabilize supplies of basic food and feed grains.

Henry A. Wallace, then secretary of agriculture, spoke of an "ever-normal granary" which would be filled with grain in bumper crop years and emptied during years of crop failure. Mr. Wallace, who is a devout student of the Bible, liked to compare his ever-normal granary plan with the Biblical Joseph's plan for the seven fat and the seven lean years in ancient Egypt. He proposed that supplies of corn, wheat, cotton, and possibly other crops be accumulated as a reserve against crop failure or against unusual requirements. Price support loans would enable farmers to hold corn on their farms for use as feed in case of shortage. Similarly, loans on wheat and cotton in warehouses and elevators would build up a safe backlog of these crops.

Mr. Wallace contemplated an adjustable price support level, so that the ever-normal granary could be managed soundly. This concept was incorporated in the farm act of 1938. However, it did not get a real trial before World War II struck.

Fairly substantial reserves were built up in the late thirties even with price support loans below 75 per cent of parity. In the fall of 1941 the carryover of corn amounted to 645 million bushels, and in the following summer the carryover of wheat amounted to 631 million bushels. These reserves would not seem large nowadays, but at that time they seemed huge, and the farm politicians were worried about "surpluses."

The reserves were depleted rapidly during the war. Within one year, stocks had fallen so sharply that all talk of surpluses ceased. The officials responsible for the wartime food program would have been glad to see much larger reserves on hand. Luckily, the North American continent was favored with uniformly good weather during the war years, and crop yields were high. But the United States was largely on a hand-to-mouth basis in basic grain supplies throughout the war and early postwar years. This experience has made farmers and farm leaders more conscious of the need for reserves.

The rule of thumb definition of a surplus of corn or wheat has increased by several hundred million bushels since pre-World War II days. In the thirties a wheat carryover of more than 200 million bushels was looked upon as excess. A corn reserve larger than 400 million bushels also was considered dangerous. Even after the experience of the bad droughts in the early thirties, agricultural policy was based on the assumption that the total grain carryover should be kept under 600 or 700 million bushels. But the heavy claims on United States grain supplies during World War II, the postwar relief and recovery years, and the Korean war caused some reorientation of opinion about carryovers.

When high price supports were continued during the ten years after World War II, the government acquired much larger amounts of grain and cotton than before the war. But the public and agricultural officialdom were not as alarmed as they might have been without the wartime experience.

Agriculture Secretary Ezra Benson and other conservative farm politicians retain their fear of surpluses. In fact, Benson and the Republican administration have used alarmism over excess supplies as their main talking point in favor of a lower price support level. During the 1952-56 debates on farm policy Mr. Benson often gave the impression that he considered the government-held surplus stocks the *only* farm problem. Some of his backers implied that the government should not worry about reserves but should allow the free market to handle this function. The best "reserve," it was said by one Farm Bureau leader, is the ability to produce rather than supplies stored above ground. Other students of farm affairs, however, have adopted a different attitude toward stockpiling basic crops. There is truth in the statement that the best reserve is ability to produce. But it is also true that government accumulation of a stockpile can help even out the flow of food products to market. This was proved both in the drought years of 1933-36 and during the early war years. In both periods grain and livestock prices would have fluctuated more drastically if the nation had not been able to draw upon reserves built up under the crop loan programs.

The agricultural committee of the National Planning Association issued a pamphlet in 1951 which tentatively suggested that reserves of 600 million bushels of wheat and "between 500 million and 1 billion bushels" of corn would not be excessive under conditions of the 1950's. The pamphlet pointed out that even a billion bushels of corn would be only about half the amount of underproduction that might result from a run of crops as bad as those of 1933-36.

As of 1956 the federal government had not established a firm policy with respect to basic food and feed reserves. Congress has juggled the carryover figures to be used in calculating price supports under the flexible parity system. But this juggling has been for the purpose of raising price guarantees rather than for the purpose of establishing safe re-

CHART 10. Carryover of Major Farm Commodities

Wheat (MIL. BU.)	Cotton (THOUS. BALES)	Corn (MIL BU.)	Food Fats & Oils (MIL LBS.)

1,080

14,700

1,022

11,200

9,720

902

1,150

1,029

562

920

5,605

769

1,608

487

962   775

256

1,589

2,789

880

| 1952 | '54 | '56 | 1952 | '54 | '56 | 1952 | '54 | '56 | 1952 | '54 | '56 |

CROP YEARS BEGINNING WHEAT JULY 1; COTTON AUG 1 CORN, OCT 1 FATS AND OILS, OCT 1 HEIGHT OF BARS ARE PROPORTIONAL TO VALUE
1956 EARS BASED ON PROSPECTS FOR PRODUCTION AND DISAPPEARANCE AS OF OCTOBER, 1955

U S DEPARTMENT OF AGRICULTURE   NEG 80 56(5) AGRICULTURAL MARKETING SERVICE

serves. The Congressional technique has been to "set aside" a certain quantity of corn, wheat, and cotton to be eliminated from statistical consideration in setting price supports. This amounts to destroying, on paper, part of the surplus.

What is needed is a carefully developed plan for carrying in stockpile an agreed-upon reserve, in the same way that the nation carries strategic reserves of metals for military purposes. The exact figures used are not as important as establishing the *idea* that a reasonable carryover is in the national interest, should not be considered "surplus," and should be maintained as part of the cost of national security against war needs or drought. The figures can always be adjusted according to experience.

So much farm discussion has centered around "surpluses," especially during Mr. Benson's regime, that a prudent reserve policy gets little consideration. No matter how troublesome the large stocks of farm products might become, they

certainly are not as troublesome as serious shortages would
be. From the viewpoint of the general public interest, it is
much better to err on the side of having too much than on the
side of having too little.

It is in this frame of mind that the Congress ought to
establish a national reserve policy for agriculture. The price
support programs developed during the last twenty-five years
are, for the most part, well suited to carrying out a reserve
policy. The Commodity Credit Corporation has developed
workable administrative methods for adjusting the nation's
stockpile through commodity loans. It has also worked out
a system of physically managing the reserves, rotating stocks
in storage to prevent waste, etc.

For such basic crops as corn, wheat, and cotton, it would
seem advisable to set "target" figures on reserves which the
C.C.C. would attempt to maintain during average crop years.
In the case of wheat, suppose this target were put at 750
million bushels. The price support loans could be maintained
at a fairly high level, say $2.25 a bushel, until the 750 mil-
lion bushel figure was reached. Then the loan would be
gradually reduced until no more wheat was being accumulated in storage.

In setting price support loan rates, the objectives would
be to stabilize market supplies and market prices and to keep
a reserve of basic crops for emergencies. During a period of
accumulation of supplies, farmers would receive higher prices
than the free market would pay. During a period of depletion
of the national granary, they would get lower prices than the
uncontrolled market would have paid. A sound ever-normal
granary program would be designed to smooth out the variations in supplies and prices from year to year. But it would
not attempt to hold prices above the long-time trend in the
free market. This was the principal mistake in price support
policy for wheat and cotton after the Korean war. The ever-
normal granary became an ever-overflowing granary.

In establishing an ever-normal granary policy for corn, the major aim is to stabilize the supply of feed for the livestock industry. Corn is primarily a raw material for meat, milk, and eggs. Only about 15 per cent goes directly into human food or industrial use. Corn is by far the most important of the feed grains—in fact, it is by far the most important of all crops in the United States in total value. Corn furnishes more than half the total feed concentrates used in the United States. Since it keeps well in storage, it serves as the stabilizing influence in the livestock industry— offsetting variations in the yield of pastures, hay crops, and other feed grains.

Corn storage policy cannot be considered separately from wheat, for wheat is also used as a feed grain. United States farmers normally feed 200 million bushels or so of wheat a year to livestock. In large measure, wheat and corn are interchangeable as livestock feed. So if the national reserve of wheat is large, not so much corn will be needed in the stockpile. But wheat cannot begin to perform the stabilizing job for the livestock industry.

The United States in recent times has used close to 3 billion bushels of corn per year as livestock feed. A reserve of 1 billion bushels of corn would be enough to last only four months. If you assume that corn has to perform the storage function for other feed concentrates, then 1 billion bushels does not seem an excessive reserve.

It is more efficient to store feed grains right on the farm where they will be fed, or in nearby small-town elevators, rather than accumulating them in large elevators in faraway cities, as in the case of wheat. The corn loan program adopted as an emergency relief measure in 1933 has turned out to be practical as a long-time ever-normal granary program.

Wartime price supports, continued nearly ten years after the war, ultimately piled up far more than necessary in the national wheat stockpile. As of 1956, in fact, more than a full year's supply was on hand! Prudent stabilization policy called for a lower price support and a lowering of the stockpile.

But the situation in corn was different. Even if some of the wheat reserve was called *feed* reserve, still the corn stockpile did not look overly large. The wartime price support level (90 per cent of parity) did not at any time result in the storage of more than a three months' supply of corn. It would seem reasonable to maintain corn loans at somewhere near the 1955-56 level, about $1.50 a bushel, until the corn reserve got up to 1.5 billion bushels. Then would be time enough to bring the corn loan down.

The main difficulty in arriving at a sensible price stabilization and ever-normal granary policy for basic crops stems from the logrolling among power blocs in agriculture. King Cotton, King Wheat, and King Corn rule Congressional farm legislative action. For years, farm lobbyists have been able to get the same treatment for these crops—the same level of price support, the same kind of acreage allotment procedure, the same sort of reserve policy (if you can call it policy). Congress never has found it possible to write programs adapted to the different conditions for each crop.

Farm lobby strength is built around the special interests of the primary areas producing corn, cotton, and wheat—the Cotton South, the midwest Corn Belt, and the Great Plains wheat states. The Farm Bureau is strong in both the South and the Corn Belt; the Farmers Union is dominant in the Great Plains. Vote trading among legislators in these areas is reminiscent of tariff bargaining in Congress. If cotton gets 90 per cent of parity guarantees, then the Corn Belt and the Great Plains must get it, too.

In the wrangling in the Senate over farm legislation in 1956, the logrolling among these groups reached a new high (or low). The administration was driving hard for continuing its flexible price support policy. The Democrats were pushing for a return to fixed guarantees at 90 per cent of parity. In an effort to "buy" southern backing for the flexible principle, Secretary Benson agreed to keep cotton price supports at a higher level in 1956 than strict interpretation of the law would allow. He wrote a letter to a southern senator saying that he would fix cotton price support at 86 or 87 per cent of parity. He also promised not to reduce cotton acreage allotments further. And he announced a huge "dumping" sale of cotton overseas to reduce the cotton surplus, which would make higher price supports possible in later years under the flexible price formula.

In order to pacify the Corn Belt, then, the Republicans wrote into the farm bill a provision increasing the corn acreage allotments above the announced figures for 1956. For wheat, a new alternative pricing plan was adopted. This plan called for a price guarantee of 100 per cent of parity on the portion of the wheat crop used for domestic food. The rest of the wheat would be supported at prices comparable with those for corn, to prevent flooding of the corn market with feed wheat.

Finally, the senators agreed to go back to the old parity formula for basic crops—which would raise the price guarantees for wheat and corn. The net effect of all this trading back and forth was that the Senate bill returned basic price supports practically to 1954 levels. In name, the flexible price support principle was maintained—but in effect, the holy symbol of 90 per cent of parity was restored to a place of honor in the Senate.

Similar examples of logrolling on acreage allotments and price supports could be drawn from Congressional debates throughout the preceding twenty-five years. Congressmen have never faced up to the economic facts which call for a different kind of price policy for corn than for wheat, a different policy for cotton than for tobacco, and so on.

In the 1950's the economic facts confronting cotton and

wheat producers could hardly have been plainer. World production had grown rapidly since the end of World War II. The need in Europe for emergency exports of these crops from the United States had vanished. United States stockpiles of wheat and cotton mounted to hitherto unheard of levels. Plainly, the situation called for lower prices and reduced production.

Under the acreage adjustment program, allotments for cotton and wheat were reduced sharply. Much of the land taken out of these crops was planted to corn, grain sorghums, and other feed crops. This was a logical adjustment to a new demand situation—less export demand for wheat and cotton and a booming demand for livestock products at home.

But price stabilization policy as directed by Congress recognized these economic signals not at all. Instead of helping the adjustment, price policy hindered it. Instead of fostering a sensible stabilization program, price policy prevented it. Congress kept price supports for all of the big three politically sensitive crops at 90 per cent of parity until 1955, and permitted only slight declines then.

These high price guarantees encouraged wheat and cotton producers to grow as much as possible on their reduced acreages, rather than put the same labor and capital resources into something else. Sensible price policy would have called for gradual reductions in both wheat and cotton supports, meanwhile keeping corn loans at 90 per cent of parity. At the same time, if Congress wanted to maintain incomes of farmers in the wheat and cotton areas at their previous level, it could have done so by means of direct subsidies not related to cotton and wheat growing. Better yet, it could have provided subsidies to help some farm families in these areas to leave farming altogether.

The use of the government loan technique for price stabilization only, instead of for raising incomes, would be a tremendous advance toward a sounder national agricultural policy. The abandonment of "equal price treatment" for the basic crops by Congress would be another long step ahead. A well-managed ever-normal granary of basic food and feed crops will not be possible until Congress is willing to grant more administrative authority in these matters.

13

Keeping Farm Income Up

If farm price supports* were used only as a tool to help level out market prices, they would not increase farm income. Over a period of years, farmers would receive about the same gross income as without the government intervention. They would benefit from the diminution of risk, lower cost, and the improved functioning of the market. The choices of consumers and the export market would be more accurately reflected in adjustments of farm output. Capricious variations in production due to lack of information and year-to-year changes in crop yields would be moderated. But forward price guarantees and supply-regulating storage programs, such as we talked about in the preceding two chapters, would not "get at" the problem of chronic low farm income because of oversupply. Nor would they prevent sharp reductions in farm income caused by industrial depression or declines in foreign demand.

In short, price supports used in this fashion would only make the free market work better in the short run and would not change significantly the distribution of the national income between farmers and nonfarm people.

If the incomes of farm people are to be brought up more nearly on a par with the incomes of the rest of us, therefore, something besides price stabilization will have to be done.

Several things have been done in the past with this goal in mind, and several things are being done today. In fact, the aim of the price support programs has been to increase income, rather than merely to stabilize prices. But added all

* Including crop loans, purchases, and direct payments in lieu of price supports—in other words, all types of guarantees to farmers based on price per unit of product.

together, these efforts have done very little to redress the balance between farm and nonfarm incomes. After more than two decades of government programs designed to raise farm income, the ratio between farm and nonfarm income per person remains about what it was at the start. To some people this means that it is futile for the government to try to improve the relative position of farmers. But it could mean that the government has been doing the wrong things.

The theoretical foundation underneath most of our "farm relief" attempts has been that of monopoly control of production and prices. Farm leaders have been fascinated with the idea that they could obtain control over their production through the government and thus extract a monopoly return in the market. They saw that manufacturers could regulate production and price—so why not farmers?

But monopoly control over farm production has been difficult to obtain. Government attempts to set prices above the free market, without adequate control over production, have created surpluses. Control of acreage alone has proved inadequate. And controls have been limited to a few basic crops. Producers of the basic crops have been helped by the price supports, to be sure, but producers of livestock, livestock products, vegetables, fruits, and most other foods have been helped very little if at all. About 75 per cent (in value) of the products of American farms have been untouched or touched only slightly by the major control and price support programs.

Conceivably, if the control programs were carried out more rigorously to cover more crops and livestock, they could be made to work. Of course, this would require individual farm quotas for a great many different products. A farmer would be given a quota in pounds of pork, pounds of beef, pounds of milk, bushels of corn, bushels of soybeans, and so on. This would require a stupendous planning of farm production from the top down. It would substitute the decisions of government officials for the decisions of individual operators of nearly 5 million separate farm enterprises. It would freeze agriculture into rigid patterns which soon would bear little relationship to the free choices of consumers for food and fiber.

Even if farmers were to accept this kind of rigid control, which is extremely unlikely, it would be a very bad proposition for the general public. It would mean a slowing down, if not a halt, in advancing productivity per man in agriculture. Any imaginable system of production control that would work would have to be based on a historical pattern of some kind, just as the crop acreage allotments have been based on the crop history of the farm. Allotments or quotas would become something like licenses to produce a particular crop or livestock product. This already has happened in the case of tobacco. In tobacco-growing regions the acreage allotment has been capitalized into the value of the land. This tends to hold production on the same farms and to prevent change in the tobacco growing pattern. Cotton acreage allotments, also, to some degree have held cotton production in the states of the Old South, even though new technology has greatly lowered costs of cotton production in the irrigated areas of Arizona and California. Imagine what a set of quotas on livestock and all crops would do to the ever-changing map of American agriculture! Consumers have much more to lose from this stoppage of change in agriculture than they do from the high prices which might immediately result from monopoly controls.

To the extent that monopoly control methods were successful in increasing farm income they would hold people in farming. But anything that stopped the movement of people from farms to cities would tend to reduce the income per person in farming, because of higher birth rates on farms. It would then become necessary to devise some way of licensing farmers instead of merely assigning quotas and allotments to farms. You cannot have freedom of entry into agriculture and still maintain a monopoly control system.

The plain facts of the matter are that agriculture is an industry which does not lend itself to centralized decision making, with administrative controls over production and prices. This is shown by the gross inefficiency of agriculture in the Soviet Union, and its failure to make rapid progress. It is shown by our own experience with tentative and partway controls. If this is so, then must agriculture reconcile itself to much lower income per person than other industries? Not necessarily.

The simplest and most direct way of bringing farm incomes into line with nonfarm incomes would be for the government to pay farm people an outright subsidy. This could be done by special lower income tax rates or higher exemptions, by checks from the federal treasury, or by many other methods. Such open subsidies have many points in their favor. They would be easier to administer, would be plainly visible to the general public, and would not interfere with the normal functioning of the competitive market system in agriculture.

Such direct subsidies are used to keep American shipping firms afloat in competition with the maritime services of other countries. Direct subsidies to keep American agriculture healthy, to attract enterprising and capable people into farming, and to assure bountiful supplies of cheap food surely are as justifiable as subsidies to the maritime industry.

Such payments to farmers, however, would have to meet the same objection as does any other form of subsidy, direct or indirect, in that they would tend to keep people in farming who are not needed there and could serve the total economy better in nonfarm work. On the basis of the per capita income figures published by the federal government, however, agriculture could be paid a considerable subsidy and still not enjoy such high incomes as to stop the movement of people to other industries.

Though outright payments from the government would be simplest, cheapest, and least disrupting to the individual enterprise and competitive market system, few politicians will advocate such a thing, and there is not the remotest possibility of such a subsidy's being enacted in the near future. Although farmers complain about their disadvantageous position in a modern, administered economy, they would turn down overwhelmingly direct handouts of this nature from the government. They may accept soil conservation payments and even payments on price guarantees for livestock, but they would hate to be in a position of taking "relief" grants.

Yet when you come down to analyzing the economics of the situation, and realize that government control and collective bargaining on prices will not do the job, then you see that direct subsidies from the government are the only way to pull farm family income up nearer to nonfarm income.

Direct subsidies to farmers can be made more acceptable both to the tax-paying public and to farm people themselves if the payments are made in return for some kind of performance by farmers. The payments to farmers for performing certain agricultural conservation practices have been popular with both farmers and nonfarmers. The logic behind this acceptance is that farmers are performing a service in the public interest by preserving national soil resources. This suggests a method for possible future expansion.

Congress would be doing far more to help agriculture if it tripled or quadrupled the present conservation payments program than it would by keeping price supports at a high level. Moreover, the conservation payments would not create surpluses; in fact, if the payments were attractive for such practices as establishing timber tracts, permanent pasture, and other nonintensive uses of land, the effect might be to lower total agricultural output slightly. This line of reasoning is behind the so-called "soil bank" plan which was passed by Congress in 1956. The only action necessary to make this program a real income support program would be to increase the amounts of the federal contributions.

A federal payment program of this character ought to be coupled with a corresponding payment program to farm families who want to leave agriculture and get established in urban occupations. It would be foolish to make farming so attractive, by means of government payments, that the normal movement off farms ceased. In the long run the most effective action the government can take in behalf of agriculture is to expedite the transfer of farm people to other occupations by means of education, employment services, and grants and aids to encourage people to leave farming.

Direct subsidies to farmers, either for the performance of soil conservation practices or for nothing at all, could be made adjustable according to some general index of business activity or farm prices. That is, the payments could be made to take up the slack when farm income through the market place sagged. During World War II and during the Korean war there was no justification for income subsidies to agriculture. The demand for farm products was strong enough for most commercial farmers to be able to make acceptable incomes without any help from government. However, when export demand fell off and farm prices collapsed, there was nothing a farmer could do to maintain his income against forces beyond his control driving it down.

Such compensatory income payments to farmers in time of industrial recession or loss of foreign markets could be logically justified as part of the nation's general economic stabilizing machinery—as unemployment compensation for non-farm workers is.

Direct subsidies would loom larger in the federal budget than price support costs, though the total cost (taxes and food costs) to the nonfarm public of maintaining a given level of farm income probably would be less. For that reason, they are not likely to be adopted in the near future as a general farm income support measure. The American public apparently believes that government payments are more "socialistic" or more disruptive of private capitalism than indirect subsidies like price support programs or the tariff. Yet payments to farmers would be more conservative of the decentralized decision-making system than elaborate controls and government price-fixing above free market levels. With a payment system, prices would be free to reflect changes in demand and supply. Farmers would be free to grow what they pleased and to sell as they pleased. The incentives to produce efficiently and market efficiently would remain as strong as ever. Direct payments to support farm income also would be much less of an interference with foreign trade than price supports used to boost income. (More about that in the next chapter.)

Another way to protect farm income without detailed controls over production, and without government fixing of prices above the market, would be to subsidize the consumption of food. Various schemes have been suggested for this, and some have been tried in a small way.

The food stamp plan was in operation from 1939 to 1943. Families on relief or receiving public assistance were given blue stamps with which they could buy foods declared in surplus. Persons receiving this subsidy had to buy orange stamps to cover their normal food purchases at regular prices. The blue stamps were issued ordinarily at the rate of fifty cents' worth for each dollar's worth of orange stamps. Thus the blue stamps would provide additions to the normal diet. In actual operation, however, many of the orange stamps were used for soap and other nonfood items in the groceries. So part of the subsidy did not go into better diets.

At its peak in 1940, about 3,970,000 people received this

food aid. The average subsidy to each individual was forty dollars a year. This program was conceived and operated more for disposal of surpluses of certain foods than for improvement of nutrition. It dwindled away when surpluses were no longer a problem.

The best-known food subsidy program in the United States is the school lunch program. It has been generally popular. The federal government furnishes foods to local agencies for providing nourishing lunches for school children. Most Americans agree that all children should have a right to good food even if their parents cannot afford it. We may think it "socialistic" to do this for grownups, but we are willing to do it for children.

This program has been gradually expanding—in the middle fifties by the addition of a special milk subsidy for schools. The chances are that this method of subsidizing food consumption will continue and grow, even during prosperous times, more as a national nutrition measure than as a farm relief measure. It has broader educational values than just teaching children themselves. The youngsters go home from a good lunch to help educate their parents on what balanced meals should contain.

The same kind of supplementary food program can be adapted to other groups. During the war many factories supplied workers with a good mid-day meal or a breakfast, and some continued this during peacetime. Public subsidy for this sort of thing would be easy to arrange and probably would increase the demand for food somewhat. However, it would be difficult to prevent people getting subsidized lunches from cutting down on their regular food spending and using the extra cash for other things.

England maintained a large food subsidy program for a long time, using special ration stamps. The British also have had infant welfare stations that distribute milk, cod liver oil, orange juice, and other foods, as well as supplementary foods for expectant and nursing mothers and pre-school-age children of low-income families.

The most far-reaching plan of food subsidy yet proposed in the United States is the Food Allotment Plan which Senator George D. Aiken of Vermont has introduced into Congress a number of times, without success. The Food Allotment Plan has two aims: to improve nutrition by making it possible for low-income families to buy a good diet, and to improve farm incomes by enlarging and stabilizing the demand for food.

Under this plan the food-purchasing power of low-income families would be increased by issuing them coupons. These coupons would be spent in grocery stores like money. The grocery stores would turn the coupons in to the government and get full cash value. In this respect the plan is like the old food stamp program.

But unlike the food stamp program, this plan would make coupons available to anyone who wanted to buy them. The stamps would be issued in units designed to provide a good diet for one person. To get them, a family would have to turn over 40 per cent of its income. For this amount, any family could enjoy a good diet—regardless of food prices and regardless of its level of pay.

The "good diet" would be determined by food scientists and would embrace as many foods as possible to allow for differences in tastes. Suppose this diet came to $5 a week. For a family of four, coupons would be worth $20 a week. A family with income of less than $50 a week would benefit by buying the coupons—providing it wanted to spend as much of 40 per cent of its income for food.

The 40 per cent figure was suggested in the Aiken bill because several surveys have shown that low-income families with fairly good diets spend about that proportion of their incomes for food.

This plan would make it possible for any family to have a good diet, regardless of income, so long as the supplies were available. Poverty would no longer be a reason for poor diets. In effect, the United States would guarantee all its citizens the right to good food.

The government administrator in charge of the food allotment plan would have power to determine amounts and kinds of foods in the allotment. He could vary the proportions of similar foods according to supplies available. For example, he might increase the amount of pork in a year of heavy hog slaughter and lower the amount of beef. Or he might increase the amount of potatoes and cut rice, wheat, or other starchy foods. The administrator also could change the makeup of the allotment if new nutritional knowledge made it advisable. However, the administrator could designate only a portion of the stamps for special foods—not more than one-third of them. This is to prevent the program from becoming a surplus disposal scheme and to permit a wide freedom of choice by families participating in the plan.

Any family could apply for participation by submitting two statements of fact—the number of persons in the family and the total family income. Short forms could be used. Spot checking of these forms would be necessary, as in the case of income taxes, to avoid excessive evasions.

To prevent the program from reducing incentives to work, an unemployed man from sixteen to sixty-five who is not in school or disabled would have to show that he is registered for work and provide proof that he had not turned down suitable work within the last six weeks. As a further safeguard, no one could buy the coupons for less than 25 per cent of their value, no matter how low his income. If he had insufficient income even to pay that much, then he would have to go on out-and-out relief.

This kind of program of course would increase total national spending for food. Surveys by the United States Department of Agriculture have shown clearly that people will buy and use enough food for good nutritional standards if they can afford to do so. A survey in 1948 found that families with incomes from $1,000 to $2,000 per year spent an average of $884 for food. Those with incomes between $4,000 and $5,000 averaged $1,560 for food. The families in the $4,000-to-$5,000 bracket averaged larger than the families in the $1,000-to-$2,000 bracket. If an adjustment for family size is made, the food expenditures of the higher-income families would average around $1,300 a year, compared with $884 for the lower-income families. In the $1,000-to-$2,000 bracket the average family was spending about 45 per cent of its income for food. In the higher bracket the average family spent 32 per cent.

This survey information would seem to indicate that government expenditures on a food allotment plan would go mostly to increase the total national spending on food. However, controls would be necessary to prevent people from using their food allotment coupons for other things than food in the grocery stores, which sell almost everything these days. This should not be an impossible job of administration.

How much would such a program cost the government? That would depend, of course, on the state of prosperity and the amount of unemployment. During a severe depression the government would be paying out large amounts of money —probably on the order of 2 to 4 billion dollars a year. If that were looked upon as a farm subsidy alone, it probably would frighten Congress away. However, if it were considered as part of a general antidepression program and as a national nutrition measure, it might be acceptable. In times of prosperity, expenditures for a food allotment program would be much smaller. One estimate of the effects in 1955, a year of high national income, places the cost to the federal government at around 700 million dollars.

How much of this extra spending for food would come back to farmers? Farmers get about 40 to 50 per cent of the consumer's food dollar, so it is reasonable to assume that they would get at least that proportion of the new spending. They might get considerably more.

Margins taken by processers, handlers, and distributors of food products are relatively fixed. If we assume that supplies of farm products remained unchanged, the marketing agencies would not be handling any bigger quantities, so they probably would not increase their share very much. Ordinarily, an increase in demand for food would be accompanied by an increase in marketing margins, because wages and other marketing costs would be going up too. But in this case the government would be increasing the total demand for food with no corresponding increases in marketing costs.

Some economists even believe that farmers' incomes might be increased more than the amount of the government subsidy. Here is the line of reasoning, again assuming that the total supply of food does not change:

For the nation as a whole, consumers spend about the same proportions of their incomes for food year in and year out. But this pattern covers up some wide differences among income groups. The lower-income families vary their food buying considerably when their incomes rise and fall, or when prices change, because they are always close to the margin on necessities. When their incomes drop off, or prices go up, they have to cut down on food—since that is the only place they can cut. Higher-income families, though, tend to consume about the same amount of food all the time—they have enough margin over necessities to cut spending somewhere else and keep on eating well.

If the government poured a large amount of money into the hands of low-income families, with the string attached that it be spent only for food, this would have two important effects on total food spending: (1) It would help level out ups and downs in food spending, because it would stabilize the demand for food of the people who cause most of the ups and downs. (2) It would cause the upper income groups to spend higher proportions of their incomes for food. The low income groups would be taking a greater share of the total food supply than they did before, thus leaving less available to the upper income groups. But the upper-income families would continue to demand as much as they had before and would bid up prices to get it. In order to get as much as before, they would have to bid farm products away from nonfood uses, waste, and export.

In other words, food prices would rise more from an injection of purchasing power into the low income groups than from an injection evenly distributed over the whole population.

The increase in national food spending from a nutrition subsidy program would not be evenly distributed among farmers. It would go mainly to the farmers producing foods needed to improve our diets. The Department of Agriculture once estimated that about two-thirds of the increase would go for dairy products. Most of the remainder would go for leafy green and yellow vegetables, meat and poultry, and tomatoes and citrus fruit—in that order of importance. There would be small increases in spending for other vegetables and fruit, eggs, potatoes, and sweet potatoes. Farmers producing grain would profit indirectly from an increased demand for feed from livestock producers.

There are many objections to the food allotment plan, which is why the plan has not been adopted. The major farm organizations, except the Farmers Union, have never been enthusiastic about food subsidies other than the school lunch program. Farm leaders believe food subsidies would encourage a "cheap food philosophy" which in the long run would damage farmers' interests. They would prefer to try to figure out government programs which will enable farmers to get higher incomes "through the market," without large government outlays which are visible to the nonfarm public.

Some social workers dislike the food allotment plan because they say there is no reason to treat food as a special good above all others. They think food allotments would limit freedom of consumer choice as between food and other goods. They prefer the approach of a national social security program which would provide for a minimum standard of living in money. The consumer could spend the money for food or for betting on the horses or for clothing—whatever he wanted. These social workers believe that a social stigma attaches to coupons but not to a government security check.

Some people also argue against the allotment plan on the grounds that it would discourage home production of food. Families who are guaranteed a minimum diet would not be likely to put in extra work on a garden. Administration of a food allotment program would be difficult, admittedly. It would be hard to be certain that family income reports were accurate. Where several people in the family are working, there would be a chance for graft. But this is true also of income tax reports, and food allotments probably could be handled as efficiently as tax collections.

Any method of providing farmers with more income than they can obtain through the free market system has some objections. The method you choose depends on your evaluation of the different objections.

So far, in the United States we have preferred to tinker with the market pricing machinery, to regulate acreage, to control marketings, and that sort of thing. In other words, we have preferred to interfere with the farm economy *in detail*, rather than to pay out government subsidies on a large scale for soil conservation or for food consumption. The subsidy programs would permit prices to move freely and to guide consumers in their decisions. They would permit a greater degree of freedom in individual farm decisions on production and marketing than present farm programs.

Maybe some day we will decide that it is better to let the individual enterprise farm economy operate freely than it is to try to lace it into a strait-jacket of monopoly controls. When that decision is made, direct payments to farmers or a general food subsidy will seem more attractive than they do now. For such methods are more consistent with free enterprise than production controls and price fixing.

14

Farmers and World Trade

In the debate in the United States Senate on the Tariff Bill of 1824, Robert Y. Hayne of South Carolina declared, "It [the tariff] threatens us with the total loss of our markets for cotton, rice and tobacco. . . . If we do not buy British manufactures, she cannot be our customer for the products of our country." John Randolph of Virginia made the same point more explosively, and threatened southern defiance of a federal tariff law: "If, under a power to regulate trade, you prevent exportation; if, with the most approved spring lancets you draw the last drop of blood from our veins; if, *secundum artem*, you draw the last shilling from our pockets, what are the checks of the Constitution to us? A fig for the Constitution! When the scorpion's sting is probing to the quick, shall we stop to chop logic?"

The Tariff Bill of 1824 was passed, nevertheless, over the objections of the agricultural South. It established Henry Clay's "American System" of protective tariffs for the manufacturing industries of the North. It played an important part in creating the deep antagonism between the agricultural South and the industrial North, which later led to the southern doctrine of nullification and undoubtedly contributed to the tensions which brought on the Civil War.

The issue drawn by Hayne and Randolph in 1824 has been a hot one throughout American history. It is a simple issue. Trade regulations which reduce the sales of foreigners in the United States inescapably reduce foreign purchases of United States goods and services. Foreigners can buy here only with United States dollars. To obtain dollars they must earn them by selling goods or services to Americans. Foreign trade, like any kind of trade, is, to use Stuart Chase's phrase, "stuff for stuff." This does not imply that trade in goods and services must balance exactly year by year as in barter. Loans, investments, and gifts of money may permit large surpluses of either exports or imports for long periods. During the nineteenth century the United States borrowed heavily from Europe and was able to import more goods than it exported. As these loans were paid off, we exported more than we imported. Then, during the last forty years we have made huge loans and gifts to foreign countries which have permitted us to continue to export more than we have imported. But the movement of international credits does not change the fundamental rule that a barrier which restricts imports also restricts exports. Any tariff which benefits one industry thus inevitably injures other industries. There can be little doubt that American exports of farm products would be larger today if foreign producers could sell more freely in the rich American market.

Naturally, industries which face competition from overseas want government protection against that competition, usually by tariffs or trade quotas. Naturally, also, industries which depend heavily on export sales oppose tariffs which cut the purchasing power of their customers. That is the heart of the trade policy issue.

The heavy Republican majorities among midwestern farmers during the many years when the Republican party stood for high tariffs are difficult to explain in this context. Midwestern agriculture depended heavily on exports of wheat, pork, and lard, and still does. High tariffs are damaging to these exports. Iowa, Illinois, and Kansas farmers logically should have voted Democratic like the South. Yet they stayed loyal to the G.O.P. Republican congressmen saw to it that high duties were imposed on grains and meat, along with manufactured products. Apparently, many farmers thought a tariff on wheat or corn would protect their prices, as the politicians said.

CHART 11. Value and Volume of U.S. Agricultural Exports

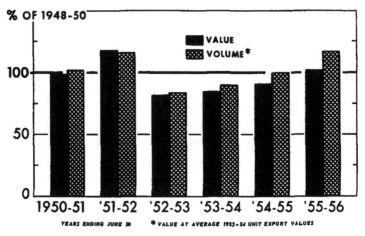

U. S. DEPARTMENT OF AGRICULTURE   NEG. 3616–56 (10)   AGRICULTURAL MARKETING SERVICE

But of course a tariff offers no protection to producers of a product that is exported in large quantity and not imported. The United States never imported a significant amount of meat, lard, or grain without a tariff, so how could a tariff provide any protection? United States prices have been below world prices because of greater production efficiency. So tariffs on wheat, corn, lard, or meat are practically meaningless, regardless of their height. (When American prices are pegged above world levels by government action, however, some kind of import control becomes necessary.)

An Iowa congressman campaigning for reelection in 1932 claimed that the tariff of 25 cents a bushel on corn was helping farmers by protecting them against imports. This was at a time when corn prices were around 12 or 15 cents a bushel!

The effect of the protective tariff on the midwestern farmer actually has been to increase the costs of the manufactured goods he buys and to lower the prices of the things he sells.

Perhaps midwestern farmers continued to vote for high-tariff candidates not because they were high-tariff candidates but because they were Republicans and represented the party that led the Union to victory in the Civil War. At any rate, this propensity of theirs to favor an economic policy very damaging to their own interests has become a classic historical example of irrational voter behavior from the economic viewpoint.

Conflicts over foreign trade policy no longer are so clearly along the lines of North against South or manufacturing against agriculture. Today, the lines of special interest in foreign economic policy are mixed. The South, now that it has gone heavily into cotton textile manufacture as well as production of the raw cotton, no longer stands solidly against protectionism and for free trade. The North, now that many of its most efficient industries depend heavily on sales to other countries, no longer stands solidly for protective tariffs. Agriculture is torn and divided on matters of foreign trade policy. Some commodity groups, such as the cotton growers, still throw their weight toward policies encouraging imports into the United States. But other farm groups are highly protectionist.

Five of the politically sensitive "basic" crops—cotton, wheat, corn, tobacco, rice—are export crops. Producers of these crops, and of hogs (which are so closely tied to corn), have a large stake in freer world trade. Yet, if one were to generalize for agriculture as a whole, he would have to say that the policies advocated by the major farm groups have been nationalistic and restrictive of foreign trade. The agricultural programs of the United States since 1933 generally have been of this character. This is true despite the fact that two major farm organizations, the Farm Bureau and the Farmers Union, have consistently advocated freer foreign trade and have supported the reciprocal trade agreements program aimed at lowering trade barriers. But while the general farm organizations have been issuing high-sounding statements about free trade, special commodity groups within these catch-all organizations have lobbied effectively for tariffs and quotas on their products.

Moreover, the price support and acreage control programs on basic crops have been in direct conflict with a freer foreign trade policy. When prices of our main export products, such as wheat, cotton, soybeans, and tobacco, are kept at a high level by government action, this makes it more difficult for foreigners to buy them, obviously. When prices of products which we import, such as sugar, wool, and some dairy products, are kept above world price levels by government action, then the United States must establish import barriers against foreign shipments of these goods. If it did not, the American government would be supporting prices for the whole world.

In spite of its high price support policy, the United States has continued to export large amounts of wheat, cotton, and other farm products. This has been possible only by subsidies of various kinds. Immediately after the war, we gave these products away through relief programs in Europe and Asia. And under the Marshall Plan and Mutual Security program we continued to finance large shipments of farm products overseas. Agricultural exports soared to new highs. In the years 1945 to 1948 the United States exported better than 300 million bushels of wheat a year, for example, as compared with only about 56 million bushels a year in the 1935-39 period. In 1951-52, wheat exports averaged 475 million bushels a year!

After 1952 our foreign aid programs were reduced. Most of the dollar subsidies to other countries since then have been used for military equipment or for machines to make military equipment. This change in the nature of our aid

CHART 12. U.S. Has Smaller Share of World's Wheat Export Market

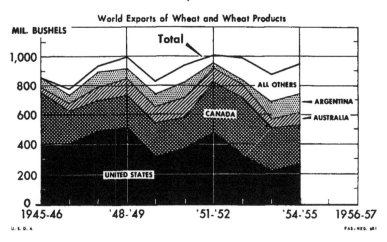

World Exports of Wheat and Wheat Products

U. S. D. A   FAS-NEG. 681

CHART 13. U.S. Exports of Cotton Decline as Foreign Production Increases

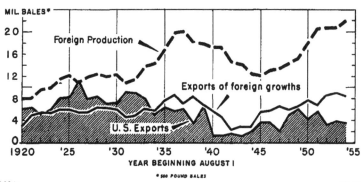

U. S. D. A.   NEG. 439A

programs had a striking effect on exports of important agricultural products. Exports of wheat and flour in 1954 and 1955 were only about half as large as in the 1948-52 period. Exports of cotton also were sharply lower.

The drop in exports was not entirely a consequence of the decline in aid to other countries. Part of it was due to the recovery of agriculture in Europe and Asia from the effects of the war. In addition, high price supports for wheat, cotton, corn, rice, and other products in the United States encouraged foreign countries to increase production of these commodities. Unquestionably, a major reason for the expansion of cotton exports from Mexico and Pakistan, for example, has been the high prop under American cotton prices. It has been easy for other countries to undersell America in the world cotton market. It would be difficult for the United States to sell farm products in today's world market even without the handicap of a high price support program. Most countries prefer to use their scarce dollars for buying certain American industrial products which they cannot get so easily elsewhere. They prefer to buy standardized farm products such as wheat and cotton in countries where they can use nondollar currency.

To maintain farm exports since the reduction in foreign aid programs, the government has used other forms of subsidy and gifts. Other countries that export farm products resent these subsidies as "dumping," as do farmers in the countries receiving cut rate wheat or cotton. And export subsidies are not likely to be very effective in the long run, anyway, because other countries take measures to restrict subsidized sales in their markets. The United States applies countervailing duties to nullify foreign dumping programs. So we should not expect any different action from other countries.

There are only two ways, fundamentally, that the United States can recover and hold foreign markets for agricultural products. One is to drop price support levels so that export prices are competitive with those of other countries. The other is to make it possible for foreign countries to earn dollars more easily.

This means lower tariffs, higher trade quotas, and a simplified system of customs to make our American market more penetrable. Present customs regulations are so cluttered up with red tape that it often takes three or four years for a foreign businessman to find out what tariff classification his goods come under so that he knows what duty he will have to pay.

The relationship of foreign trade to the farm problem has been a keynote of farm discussion since the end of World War I. The first farm relief proposals of the early twenties were nearly all attempts to insulate farm prices from the world market and thus were nationalistic in their approach. Many of them originated with Republican farm leaders of the Midwest and Great Plains states, and they rode on the assumption that the protective tariff, which had been a part of the American economic system for a century, was here to stay. In fact, the proposals were often promoted under the slogan of "making the tariff effective for agriculture."

One set of farm plans (there were several variations: the McNary-Haugen plan, the export debenture plan, etc.) would have established a two-price system for the major export crops. The proportion of each crop used for domestic consumption would be priced at a "parity" level, while the export surplus would be sold in the world market for whatever it would bring.

Another approach was to reduce production to make up for the loss in export volume. Every farmer would be given a "domestic allotment" of acreage, the production from which presumably could be sold at a parity price.

Some farm leaders and many agricultural economists pointed out that the principal villain in the farm surplus picture was the protective tariff. Instead of trying to adjust agriculture, they said, we should slash tariff rates. They argued that the United States had become a great creditor nation and needed to import more in order to receive payment on its foreign debts and to provide dollar purchasing power for the buyers of American exports. They argued that if the American tariff could be sharply reduced, many of the low-price problems of cotton, wheat, lard, and tobacco producers would disappear.

These two contradictory approaches to the farm problem met head on in the New Deal. Cordell Hull, the secretary of state, successfully put over his idea for reciprocal trade agreements. Congress passed the Reciprocal Trade Act in 1934, giving the president power to adjust tariff duties by agreement with foreign countries. Meanwhile, Agriculture Secretary Henry A. Wallace was launching the Agricultural Adjustment Administration, with its controls over crop acreage, in an attempt to reduce agricultural production to a point closer to the size of the domestic market. The aim of the trade agreements program was to reverse, or at least modify, a worldwide trend toward economic nationalism. The aim of the A.A.A. program was to fit American agriculture to a world of economic nationalism and little trade.

Henry Wallace himself was a strong advocate of lower tariff barriers and expanding world commerce. He conceived of the A.A.A. program as a stop-gap to protect farm incomes until world trade could again absorb all the export surpluses of American farms. In his book *New Frontiers*, published in 1934, he wrote as follows:

"If the president of the United States, using the tariff powers of 1934, can move forward slowly yet steadily toward reciprocal arrangements with other nations, and so make it possible for us to accept more of the goods which they produce most efficiently in exchange for the goods which we produce most efficiently, it may be possible within five or ten years to do away with much of the production control of the Agricultural Adjustment Act.

"The old-fashioned, laissez-faire economists, especially those hooked up with the big banks, the boards of trade, and the commission houses, are very enthusiastic about such possibilities. I agree with them in theory, but in practice I am wondering if it will be possible for the president to push his tariff bargaining so rapidly that foreign purchasing power will be sufficiently enlarged five or ten years hence to enable us to do away completely with agricultural control."

Mr. Wallace's fears were justified. The reciprocal trade agreements program, though it did help to expand exports of some farm products, has not been a sufficiently powerful weapon to cope with the problem of agricultural surpluses and low prices. Meanwhile, agricultural policies designed to raise prices of farm products have driven us toward nationalistic trading policies affecting farm products. This has been a source of continuing quarrels between the State Department and the Agriculture Department.

Since the end of World War II, American leaders of both political parties have been exhorting foreign countries to join us in a crusade for lower trade barriers and expanded international commerce. Congress has regularly renewed the trade agreement authority of the president, reaffirming the national policy of freer international trade. Yet time after time in these postwar years Congress, responding to pressures from special interests, has undercut the national trade policy by granting higher protection to certain industries. In many cases these have been farm commodity interest groups.

At the time of the comprehensive tariff negotiations at Geneva in 1947, a threatened rise in the American wool tariff and a proposed import quota very nearly upset the whole trade conference. The leadership for this worldwide reduction of trade barriers had come from the United States. Department of State negotiators had worked strenuously for a reduction in imperial preferences among the British Commonwealth nations. Australia was in a key position in this bargaining, and Australia wanted just one thing—a reduction in the American tariff on raw wool.

C. Addison Hickman, in a book, *Our Farm Program and Foreign Trade*, published by the Council on Foreign Relations, describes the significance of the wool tariff in this trade conference:

"While debate on the wool bill raged in congress, progress at Geneva toward the general reduction of tariff rates was virtually halted. Wool was a product which was heavily involved in world trade. Furthermore, this threat to raise the tariff on an American industry which was already heavily protected cast serious doubt upon the consistency and integrity of the United States policy. If congress should give sharply increased protection to the American wool industry, especially through such a drastic device as a quota, what assurance could other nations have that United States negotiators at Geneva had real authority?

"William L. Clayton, then under-secretary of state, flew back from Geneva to explain to legislators in Washington that the proposed raising of wool tariffs threatened to destroy a project which was at the center of United States trade policy. But farm interests prevailed; the wool bill passed in both houses. President Truman, however, saved the Geneva conference by his veto."

Many similar examples could be cited from recent American history—most of them not ending as happily for the advocates of freer world trade as in the 1947 wool tariff situation. American cane and beet sugar growers won sharply higher barriers against foreign sugar at the time of the 1947 Geneva trade conference. Cheese producers got Congress to give them stiff quotas against foreign cheese during a period when the Marshall Plan administration was advising the Danes and the Dutch to expand cheese production for export. In the Marshall Plan Act itself, farm interests achieved special treatment. The secretary of agriculture was authorized to pay up to 50 per cent of the cost of farm products declared in surplus to make them available to European countries. Of course, this was nothing but old-fashioned dumping under a new name.

Agriculture is far from being the only "sinner" in this matter. The watchmakers, the pencil manufacturers, the clothes-pin manufacturers, the tuna fishermen and briar pipe manufacturers, among others, all have "cast doubts on the integrity of American policy" at various times because of their influence in getting trade barrier protection in Congress.

The "escape clause" written into trade agreements permits an American industry to enter a complaint that it is being injured by imports and to get relief in the form of a higher tariff if the complaint is sustained. The United States Tariff Commission tends to be vulnerable (or sympathetic) to such applications for relief. Ultimately, the president must decide whether to approve or disapprove a resort to the "escape clause." Mostly, Mr. Truman and Mr. Eisenhower have decided in favor of the general interest and turned down these requests. But Mr. Eisenhower made an exception in the case of Swiss watch imports. He did so on the ground that skilled workers in the watch industry were needed for national defense and should be protected in their jobs. Nevertheless, this action cost heavily in damage to the nation's standing as a sincere advocate of freer world trade. Industries that fail to achieve tariff protection through this escape clause provision in the trade agreements often exert their influence on Congress to try to knock out the whole agreement program or to tie it up with restrictions. The majority in Congress which favors the executive agreement method for tariff making, however, has not been seriously endangered as of 1956.

Many labor unions in industries which are affected by foreign competition chime in on the demand for tariff and quota protection. The most recent major protagonist on the high-tariff side of the argument is the cotton textile industry. This industry has been suffering from an invasion of the United States market by Japanese textiles. The changed attitude of the textile manufacturers has tended to weaken the low-tariff stand of southern congressmen, historically our most passionate believers in free trade.

Looking at the history of American trade policy since World War I, one could draw the conclusion that our traditional protectionism has been reversed. A new high in protectionism was reached in the Smoot-Hawley Tariff Act of 1930. This undoubtedly was a contributing factor in the general paralysis of world trade in the early thirties. But in 1934, 110 years after the protective tariff got rooted in the United States economy, the Trade Agreements Act apparently set America on a new path in world economic affairs. Under this law American tariffs have been steadily reduced. Also, United States trade with the world has risen dramatically, but close study of the facts will show that the major factors have been the Second World War, during which we exported huge volumes of all kinds of goods to our allies under the Lend-Lease program, and the postwar economic and military aid programs. The growth of "normal" commercial trade in "real" (nonmoney) terms has been far less sensational. So far as agriculture is concerned, trade is little if any freer than it was immediately after World War I.

The arena of the battle between industries wanting import barriers and industries wanting to expand exports has been changed. It is no longer so largely confined to the halls of Congress, though that is still the main part of the arena, but also includes the State Department in its conduct of trade agreement bargaining and the Department of Agriculture in its manipulation of import quotas to back up its price support programs. To some extent this gives the general interest a stronger voice in trade policy and makes minority protectionist elements less influential. But the latter retain plenty of power, just the same.

Since a severe dollar shortage in the outside world continues to limit exports of farm products, various schemes have been employed to get farm surpluses out of the country. The latest of these is the program to take payment for exports in foreign currency. Congress authorized expenditures up to 1 billion dollars over a three-year period for this purpose. By accepting francs, pounds, lire, or other currency, the United States permits foreigners to buy without the necessity of selling to us to earn dollars.

The idea behind this program is that the United States can use foreign money to finance military bases, to buy strategic minerals, or, in some cases, to pay for technical assistance or other economic aid. To the extent that this program leads the United States to buy things from other countries that it would not otherwise buy, it helps to expand trade. To the extent that it does not do this, nothing is gained. Foreign buyers of our farm products may merely substitute these purchases for normal commercial purposes.

To the extent that the United States does not use the foreign currency at all—or merely gives it back to the recipient country for use on projects of which we approve—then the "sales" become gifts. This may often be a wise policy—but it is not "expanding export trade" in any continuing way.

The United States also has a program of undisguised gifts of farm products, authorized under the same act as is the "foreign currency sales" program. This is useful in meeting emergency food shortages in foreign lands. But it is much more difficult to give away food than many Americans think. How often we hear the comment, "America can have no surpluses when half the world doesn't get enough to eat." But the fact is that many foreign countries do not want our gifts of food and will not take them—because their own farmers resent it and because other exporting countries resent it.

Maybe more can be done to make effective use of United States food surpluses outside the commercial channels of trade. One suggestion is to establish school lunch, in-plant feeding, or food stamp programs in countries where undernourishment is serious. Safeguards would be necessary to prevent free food from replacing normal food purchases. In most needy countries government administrative services are incapable of carrying out such programs efficiently. So it might be necessary for the United States to manage them with American personnel. Whether this would be worth the cost, as a benefit either to United States farmers or to the recipient country, is dubious. But some such experimental programs ought to be tried, at least, to test the results, if a willing "laboratory" country can be found. A school lunch program for Peru, for example, has interesting possibilities as a supplement to our technical assistance programs there.

In a trading world of tariffs, export subsidies, quotas, currency exchange controls, and other trade barriers, international commodity agreements sound like a good way to bring order out of chaos. The American State Department has been favorable to this idea, and some American farm leaders have looked upon such agreements as a way of increasing exports.

For about fifteen years wheat-exporting and -importing countries tried to reach agreement on a plan within which most of the world trade in wheat would take place. A compact was finally agreed upon in March 1948. It included four exporting countries and forty importing countries. Each exporting country contracted to sell—if called upon to do so—a stated amount of wheat to member importing countries at the top limit price set in the contract. Each importing country agreed to buy—if called upon—a stated amount of wheat at the lower limit of prices in the agreement.

The wheat prices set in the agreement are not upper and lower limits on world prices. They simply represent guaranteed contract prices between buyers and sellers. If world prices fall below the agreed contract price, then importing countries have to buy the quantity agreed upon at the minimum price. If prices go above the maximums, then the exporting countries have to supply their quotas at the agreed maximum prices.

The wheat agreement covered a large part of the world's trade in wheat. It included the United States, Canada, Australia, and France. However, some large exporters, such as the Soviet Union and Argentina, have not been in the agreement.

The agreement was renewed in 1953 with some changes, but the United Kingdom, the biggest importer, did not enter. The reason was that Britain felt the guaranteed minimum price was too high in view of prospects for rising world production and the mounting surpluses in the United States and Canada. In the dickering over the new agreement, the difference finally narrowed down to about five cents a bushel, but Britain remained firm and stayed out. This illustrates the difficulty of maintaining an international agreement covering commodity prices. Britain concluded in 1953 that its interest in adequate supplies of wheat at moderate prices was protected without an agreement.

The significance of commodity agreements is the recognition by both importing and exporting countries that they have

a common interest in stable prices. Agreements are an interference with individual enterprise and free competition. But
so are tariffs and subsidies. International agreements, in
theory, should be a more orderly way to handle world trade,
and less restrictive of trade than tariffs, quotas, subsidies,
and currency exchange controls.

The wheat agreement was expected to discourage importing countries from setting up nationalistic, self-sufficiency
programs. It was expected to encourage maintenance of high
wheat production in the exporting countries by assuring
steady and reliable outlets. In practice, importing countries
have continued to subsidize their own wheat growers to a
considerable extent, and the exporting countries have been
troubled with surpluses.

Although the international commodity agreement seems
to be far from a complete solution to world trade problems,
it nevertheless has promise as a means of avoiding some of
the extremes of trade warfare. State management of foreign
trade of one kind or another probably is with us for some time
to come. International agreements seem to be a wiser way to
manage trade than the old-fashioned methods of subsidy,
quota, tariff, and exchange control. The wheat agreement has
not been a complete success, but neither has it been a complete
failure. During the years that the agreement has been in
effect, American wheat prices have been higher than the
prices in the agreement. So the United States government
has had to subsidize wheat to member importing countries.
But such subsidies do not incur the ill will of other countries,
since they are provided for by mutual agreement.

International commodity agreements, no matter how useful as a means of regularizing commerce and establishing a
more logical international division of labor for a particular
commodity, cannot by themselves greatly expand exports
of American farm products. The limiting factor still is the

supply of dollars in the outside world. Despite the most strenuous efforts to export farm products by subsidy, gift, salesmanship (the Eisenhower administration has been impressed with the possibilities of this method), and other schemes, including commodity agreements, the hard truth remains—America must import more if she wants to export more.

Major sectors of American agriculture still are heavily dependent on exports and are likely to continue to be. In their own self-interest, the producers of the major export crops should continue to use their political strength to press for lower trade barriers in general and to minimize the conflicts in domestic agricultural policy with a freer foreign trade policy.

In the larger sense, American agricultural policy must give way to the whole national interest in expanding world trade.

This does not mean that farmers must be left to shift for themselves without government help. But it means that whatever income supports are provided for farmers should be such as to interfere as little as possible with international trade. Price supports designed for stabilization purposes only, as outlined in earlier chapters, would be a great advance in this respect. It is the high price supports which, more than any other agricultural policy, have conflicted with the overall national trade policy. If farmers are to receive income supplements, beyond what they receive in the market, then those supplements should be direct and unrelated to particular commodities.

Direct subsidies, when associated with a particular product, such as the subsidy payments on wool, tend to keep producers in that business and thus to prevent foreigners from expanding their sales in the United States. The benefited producers are, in effect, given a trading advantage over their foreign adversaries. This is the situation with respect to sugar. The tariff on sugar is relatively low. But American sugar producers not only are protected by a quota system which limits sugar imports absolutely; they also get subsidy payments from the government.

It is in the interest of consumers, of course, to get goods and services from the cheapest source. Any tariff, subsidy, or quota that enables high-cost American producers to maintain a larger share of the market than they could maintain by competition injures the public at large.

The general public also has a stake in trade policies that will strengthen this nation's allies and serve its foreign policy aims. The special interest of any group of producers should never take precedence over national policies to develop a cooperative, peaceful community of nations.

These are the reasons why agricultural subsidies should be as general as possible and not associated with special commodities.

Agricultural policies which permit the free market to function effectively in guiding production and marketing are the policies best fitted to a liberal foreign trade policy.

15

The Soil

Is America in danger of running short of soil resources in the visible future?

Some people think so. Population is overtaking food production, we read in a steady flow of books and magazine articles, and the thin crust of top soil necessary for food production is being recklessly dissipated.

As I sat down to write these lines, the mail brought one of the standard releases of the Population Reference Bureau. It says 150 square miles of new farm land should go under cultivation each day to assure the world an adequate diet. Moreover, "a great many of the world's farms are eroding and deteriorating as a result of carelessness and ignorance," reports the Bureau. "In the United States alone, the annual loss of top soil from farms is placed at about 3 billion tons."

In the same mail came a release from the California Institute of Technology, quoting Dr. James F. Bonner, professor of biology, that only one-quarter of the world's people are on an adequate diet. Population is outstripping food production and the deficit is getting worse every year, says Dr. Bonner. (This may be overly pessimistic. The United Nations Food and Agriculture Organization reported that food production in the world *increased* relative to the population in 1954-55. But Dr. Bonner certainly is right in saying that most of the people of the world are inadequately nourished.)

What does Dr. Bonner suggest doing about this food situation? He says it seems impossible to increase food production more rapidly than population, so we will have to replace animal protein with plant protein. "Approximately half of our cultivated food production in the United States is fed

CHART 14. World Food Production Is Catching
Up With Population Growth

Index of World Food Production and Population

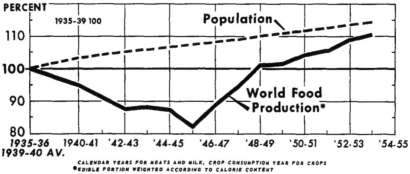

PERCENT

1935-39 100

110

Population

100

90

World Food
Production*

80

1935-36   1940-41   '42-43   '44-45   '46-47   '48-49   '50-51   '52-53   '54-55
1939-40 AV.

CALENDAR YEARS FOR MEATS AND MILK. CROP CONSUMPTION YEAR FOR CROPS
*EDIBLE PORTION WEIGHTED ACCORDING TO CALORIE CONTENT

U.S.D.A.   FAS NEG 390

to animals," says Dr. Bonner. "The animal eats only part of
the plant and what he does eat he returns to us with a caloric
yield of about 10 per cent." More direct use of plant protein
would clearly be more efficient and would increase total food
output in physical terms.

Dr. Bonner also would replace feed crops with potatoes,
sugar beets, and similar crops of higher edible content. He
would convert woody stalks and leaves of plants to edible
syrups and yeast. He would irrigate deserts by processed sea
water.

Already one of these measures of increasing the food
supply—replacement of animal protein by plant protein—
is being forced upon us, Dr. Bonner is quoted as saying.
Even in the United States, he says, within fifty years we will
have cut our meat consumption relative to plant food down
to two-thirds its present level.

This is routine. You can pick up similar predictions almost
daily. Very few of the scientists who make these calculations
stop to consider that this is far from being "one world" of
food production and distribution. Nor is there much prospect
that it will be in the near future. Some countries of the Far

East are running close to the borderline of starvation. They are proof of the doctrine of Thomas Robert Malthus that human population will press against the food supply, which is limited by the amount of land, until poverty and starvation are the common lot of mankind. But the countries of the West at the same time have disproved Malthus convincingly, especially the United States. There is evidence that some "Malthusian" countries are beginning to generate production enough to pull themselves off the brink—and not by eating wood pulp, either, but that is another story.

What I am concerned with here is the question of whether the United States is running short of soil resources. At a time when agriculture is troubled with surpluses, you would not think the scientific and pseudo-scientific scare stories about the disappearance of our soil would catch much of an audience. But they do. Fear of future food shortage makes an impact on the public even when the grain bins are overflowing. How often do you hear this expression: "Yes, we have surpluses today, but within a few years we'll have shortages." That is essentially what people like Dr. Bonner, Fairfield Osborn (*Our Plundered Planet*), and William Vogt (*Road to Survival*) are saying. They are getting their message across, because it is sensational, dramatic, and easy to understand. And it deals with life and death, always interesting subjects.

These may be reasons why soil conservation programs continue to be the most popular phase of government action in agriculture. People raise relatively few objections to paying taxes to save the national heritage of soil for future generations. Soil conservation is something everybody is "for"—like home, mother, and family. The words have a nice ring to them, and who can be opposed to conserving natural resources?

But what does "conservation" mean in connection with farm land? Some of those most enthusiastic for conservation of the soil are the vaguest about what it involves. Is soil in the same category as petroleum, coal, or other irreplaceable natural resources? Obviously not. Yet some evangelists for soil conservation have talked about "losing" farm land as though it were gone forever. The first comprehensive survey of soil erosion in the United States, made in the 1930's, indicated that more than 50 million acres of land had been practically destroyed for agricultural purposes. About 150 million acres were reported to be severely damaged and in imminent danger of total loss. The survey indicated evidence of some erosion damage on a billion or more acres. Soil conservationists still talk about the 50 million acres that have been "ruined" by soil erosion.

Their figures are arresting. But they also can be misleading. Much land that has been eroded moderately can be restored to full productivity with amazing speed if it becomes profitable to do so. It is doubtful that all the 50 million "lost" acres really are lost, considering the capabilities of modern soil technologists. If the demand were strong enough, much of this land probably could be made to grow hay and pasture crops at least. Nothing much can be done about land which has been washed away to solid rock. But subsoil of clay can be treated so as to grow crops. Soil conditioners, balanced fertilizer, and irrigation can do wonders.

The point is that most soil is not irreplaceable or indispensable. In spite of the fears that we are depleting our soil resources dangerously, the United States is using the same number of acres of cropland in the 1950's as it used in 1920— about 400 million. On this area of cropland, farm output has increased by about one-half. This has come about partly by reason of an increase in yields per crop acre of one-fourth and an increase in output per animal breeding unit of nearly one-half.

The sharp reduction in the number of horses and mules has made more food grain and forage available for food-producing livestock, thus increasing food production per acre. Also, a higher proportion of farm output comes from livestock now than thirty-five years ago. This adds a second production process and increases the value of the output per acre of cropland—though not the number of calories. This trend toward more livestock is strongly in the opposite direction from that forecast by the Malthusian prophets.

Land is not as important a factor in farm production as it once was. It has been replaced to some extent by larger additions of capital—livestock, machinery, gasoline, fertilizer, insect spray. There is no doubt that United States production of food could easily be increased another 50 per cent within a few years without adding one acre of cropland. The Paley Commission report on *Resources for Freedom* in 1952 included a summary of expert opinion on potential increases in farm productivity. Scientists in the Department of Agriculture and in the state agricultural experiment stations were asked: If all the technology now known in your line of production were applied, how much would yields per acre, or per animal unit and feed unit, be increased over those in recent years, with time enough being given for farmers to make the necessary changes? The composite answer to this question for the whole United States was 86 per cent.

John D. Black and James T. Bonnen, who prepared the 1952 report on agriculture for the Paley Commission, reviewed their figures in 1956 for the National Planning Association. They concluded that "this country will need to add no new cropland to meet all the demands for farm products that will come in 1965, or by 1975 for that matter." On the contrary, they wrote, "Technology is now making such rapid gains that the acreage of cropland needs actually to be reduced, or the equivalent of this, namely, a considerable portion needs to be diverted to more extensive uses, that is, to uses with lesser inputs and hence lower outputs per acre."

Those who are alarmed about shortages of farm land in the future can get some comfort both from the record of the last thirty-five years and from the outlook for productivity per acre as seen by agricultural scientists. This is in no sense an attempt to "debunk" the concept of soil conservation or to belittle the national programs in this field. It is only to emphasize that the United States is far from a danger point in soil resources. Moreover, most soils are not like a vein of coal, which, once it is used up, is gone forever. Soils can be maintained in an optimum state of productivity indefinitely by proper treatment and control of erosion. Or they can be allowed to deteriorate for a number of years—"mining" the soil—and then renewed by intensive treatment. The proper method of handling any piece of land from the owner's viewpoint depends on the price situation and outlook and the financial situation of the owner. But government programs representing the public interest may modify the use that would be dictated by private considerations alone. No flat rule can be laid down for each farm or each farmer. If we interpret the word "conservation" as wise use of the land, then it is not always good conservation to maintain the soil at a stable level of productivity. Sometimes it is good conservation, in this meaning of the word, to "mine" the soil for a few years. This is particularly true, of course, on flat land, where erosion is not a problem and where the soil can be easily built back to a state of high productivity.

How we use our farm land in the United States depends mainly on decisions made by 4.7 million individual farmers. We have relatively few governmental restrictions on land use, such as zoning regulations, weed control laws, irrigation and drainage laws, timber cutting regulations, and the like. By and large, a farmer can do as he pleases with his land. If he feels like growing corn in rows running up and down hill for ten years straight, thus letting most of the top soil wash away and making the job of land rehabilitation extremely difficult, there is nothing to stop him. In Britain a farmer could be removed from his farm for such abuse of the soil—in theory, at least. In practice, very few farmers have been denied the right to farm by the local committees set up to judge farming performance. But this British law illustrates a principle that might be appealing in any country where land resources are scarce. The government says to the farmer, in effect, "In return for subsidies, you are expected to take good care of the soil, which you are permitted to use in public trust. If you do not protect this national resource, you will lose your permit to farm."

Public efforts to influence the private use of farm land in the United States have been limited largely to education, plus small subsidies. Although the state agricultural Extension Services had taught soil conservation practices for many years, the present national movement for soil conservation did not really begin until the mid-1930's. Hugh H. Bennett, who was head of the Soil Erosion Service in the Department of the Interior and later the first chief of the Soil Conservation Service in the Department of Agriculture, was the number one evangelist, the man who did most to launch the drive. Bennett preached fear of scarcity. He and his fellow enthusiasts "explained" the decline of most earlier civilizations* as a consequence of soil wastage—stretching the historical facts all out of shape in most cases. But they got Congress to establish a national program of technical assistance and education on soil conservation. This program has been in operation for about twenty years now. It has had a pronounced effect on land use in the United States.

The city dweller becomes aware of the impact of this program whenever he travels through a farming area. He sees contoured fields, strip cropping, terraces and dams and ponds which were not there a few years back. Less visible effects,

* See *Topsoil and Civilization*, by Tom Dale and Vernon Carter, University of Oklahoma Press.

but equally important, have been felt in crop rotations, use of legumes, liming, fertilizing, planting of trees, etc.

The establishment of the Soil Conservation Service as a new government agency dedicated to that one task jogged the federal-state Extension Services into action, too. This has led to bickering and rivalry, but it also has increased the total amount of conservation activity.

A third agency of the Department of Agriculture also has been closely involved in soil conservation work. This is the Agricultural Stabilization and Conservation Service—formerly the Production and Marketing Administration, and before that the Agricultural Adjustment Administration. The A.S.C. pays the subsidies to farmers for carrying out certain conservation practices under the Agricultural Conservation Program (not to be confused with the Soil Conservation Service program of education and technical assistance).

The A.S.C. and S.C.S. work closely together now, although they have had their bureaucratic scraps. The S.C.S. must approve the performance of a conservation practice before the farmer can be paid.

This outburst of soil conservation effort by the federal and state governments in the years since about 1935 has been accompanied by a great deal of private organizational activity. Farm organizations, farm publications, Chambers of Commerce, the Izaak Walton League, Kiwanis Clubs, and many other groups have fostered and promoted soil conservation. During a period of sharp controversy over farm price supports and other farm policies, many groups seemed eager to "do something" for farmers in a noncontroversial area.

The soil conservation movement has had its main impetus in the simple, effective plea to "save the top soil." But an added sales argument at the start and now again in the 1950's has been that conservation farming would reduce production—and thus help the price situation.

Actually, it is pretty clear that the "conservation" programs have *increased* total farm output. Better rotations, erosion control, and water conservation have boosted yields. Also, in many general farming areas, more legumes for pasture and hay have provided better-balanced feed supplies. In Iowa, livestock production capacity has been enlarged by reducing the acreage of corn—the major feed crop and the heaviest producer of nutrients per acre. The reasons are that improved rotations have raised yields of corn—and the feed supply contains more homegrown protein.

A conservation project sponsored by the Agriculture Committee of the Des Moines Chamber of Commerce provides an excellent example of the production-increasing effects of soil conservation practices. The Chamber of Commerce pledged $3,000 for a five-year soil and water conservation project on two small watersheds northeast of Des Moines. The Iowa State College Extension Service, and the Soil Conservation Service and other agricultural agencies cooperated with the Chamber in this demonstration. The area is a typical central Iowa farming community of diversified crop and livestock production. Twenty farms were involved in the project.

Work was started on the watershed in the fall of 1949. By 1954, 1,200 acres had been contoured, and 350 acres more were strip-cropped on the contour. About 11 miles of waterways and terrace outlets were built. And on the hilliest fields, 9 miles of terraces were constructed. Pastures were limed and fertilized and seeded down, wild life areas improved, ponds built, and so on. Buying cooperatively, the farmers participating in the project obtained commercial fertilizer and other materials needed in their program.

The results in total production were impressive, as can be seen in the two accompanying tables, which show the effects of the conservation program on land use and on livestock numbers.

Land Use before and after Planning

	Acres Before	Acres After	Change Made
Cropland	2,066	2,277	+211
Permanent pasture . . .	682	455	—227
Permanent hay	0	6	+6
Woodland wildlife . . .	47	91	+44
Idle	50	0	—50
Miscellaneous	155	171	+16

Change in Livestock and Poultry Numbers

	1949	1954
Dairy cows	172	255
Dairy heifers, calves	90	147
Beef cows	25	160
Beef heifers, calves	12	86
Beef feeding cattle	95	130
Market hogs	1,223	2,033
Sheep	30	42
Lambs	67	70
Chicks	5,950	5,950*
Pullets	3,775	4,130
Hens	2,850	3,870

* Increased purchase of sexed chicks gave a greater number of pullets and hens.

Note that this conservation program resulted in an increase in cropland and a decrease in permanent pasture. In other words, it did not take land out of crop production but put more land into production. The increased feed production on the farms is reflected in the increases in livestock numbers.

The experience on this soil and water conservation project could be duplicated many times throughout the nation.

Most of the so-called "conservation" practices really are just good farming practices. In nearly all cases they are immediately profitable. They do not require a sacrifice of current income in order to preserve resources for the future, as is often the case in timber conservation, for example. It is true that erosion control helps to preserve the soil for future use—or rather continuous use. But it usually is a money-making venture for the farmer in the first few years he puts it into effect.

This being the case, a city dweller may well ask whether any subsidies for soil conservation are justified. If America is in no real danger of losing its capacity to produce food, if the nation's granaries are overloaded with surpluses, and if soil conservation practices tend to increase production, why should the federal government pay farmers for conservation?

The government does not pay farmers very much in actual cash. Agricultural conservation payments averaged about 230 million dollars a year between 1945 and 1953. The appropriation made by Congress in 1956 was 250 million dollars. In the 1953-55 period about 2.3 million farmers received payments, so this amount of money does not provide any great subsidy to each farmer.

Conservation payments have been made mostly for such practices as liming, using inorganic fertilizers, and growing green manure crops; other payments have gone for irrigation, drainage, weed control, pasture, and range practices and mechanical erosion control practices. With the exception of the last item, these are for the most part not real conservation practices—that is, they do not prevent a future diminution of productivity. If irrigation or drainage are not performed now, they can be performed at some later date with the same effect on production. The line between true conservation and better farm methods cannot be drawn clearly in all cases, but most of these "conservation" practices simply increase production from the start.

Though the Department of Agriculture has become stricter in its definition of conservation in recent years, it is no great distortion to say that the conservation payments have been a subsidy for improved current farm practices.

If the objective were the true conservation of land for future use, then payments should be made for holding land completely out of production—or for converting it to a less intensive use, such as turning cropland to permanent pasture or to forestry. The Soil Conservation Service classifies 40 million acres of cropland as unsuitable for cultivation—land which should be in permanent pasture or woodland to prevent its continued deterioration. On the other hand, the S.C.S. says 285 million acres now in pasture or woods could be safely used as cropland, if properly rotated with pasture. This gives some impression of the "scarcity" of cropland in the United States. We are actually using about 400 million acres for crops now.

In view of these facts, it would seem to be difficult to justify a large public investment in true conservation. On the contrary, it could be argued that the 87 per cent of the population not living on farms would be better off to insist on full use of the land to keep food costs down. An argument could be made for continuing the public subsidies to agricultural research, education, and "conservation" practices which step up production. The public as a whole undoubtedly has benefited richly in lower food costs from these programs for improving farm production efficiency. Why should the taxpayers pay anything for keeping land out of use or in less intensive use?

The main argument for doing so must be made on grounds other than those of conservation, namely, to reduce farm production in order to raise farmers' incomes. The society as a whole cannot afford a "depressed" agriculture which attracts only the least capable young farm people; in the long run this depletion of the human resources in agriculture would be more disastrous than losing some of our topsoil. Public assistance to farmers in adjusting production can be justified as a matter of simple fairness. After all, the over-production situation in agriculture came about partly because

of national policy decisions to expand the farm plant in wartime and in the postwar years.

But there *is* a conservation argument to be made for
public subsidies to take land out of production. The estimates
of future soil needs made by the naturalists might be *right*.
Maybe technology will *not* be able to keep pace with food
needs. Maybe all the soil we have now will be needed, plus
whatever can be restored or reclaimed from the natural state.
It might be wise not to gamble too heavily on an end to
Malthusianism. So long as the welfare of farmers calls for a
reduction in farm production anyway, there is no point in
taking any risk on future soil needs.

Establishing grass and forest cover on land not needed for
crop production and curbing erosion on all our farm lands
are in the public interest also because they help to prevent
floods, limit siltation in the rivers, and preserve the natural beauty of the lakes and streams. The Soil Conservation
Service and many private conservation agencies have fought
a long battle with the Army Engineers to get recognition for
the importance of stopping rain where it falls. Flood control
works are much more effective with a sound soil and water
conservation program protecting the watershed than without
such a program. In many river valleys, dams and levees
would be unnecessary for flood control if the farm land were
properly farmed. Small dams and reservoirs on the tribu-
taries often can obviate the need for a big dam on the main
stream.

Everything considered, there are ample reasons for continuing and enlarging greatly the national effort in soil
conservation—even though a shortage of soil does not appear
likely as far as we can see ahead. More emphasis should be
on conservation measures that will reduce total output. The
effect of the Soil Conservation Service, of the state Extension
Services, and of the Agricultural Conservation Program has
been to increase output. The Soil Conservation Service esti-

mates that about one-fourth of our farm land has now been
adequately protected by soil and water conservation practices, and the remainder is being put under conservation
farming methods at the rate of about 3 per cent a year. This
is all to the good. It has improved production efficiency of
the farmers reached. But the over-all economic effect of the
drive for conservation has been to worsen the supply picture
and drive prices lower. What is needed along with this program is a *true* conservation program for taking land out of
use or putting it to less intensive use.

This is the aim of the so-called "soil bank" program passed
by the 1956 session of Congress. For once, the major farm
organizations, Democrats, and Republicans were in agreement on this plan. It calls for the removal of farm land from
production. Farmers are given the opportunity to earn payments from the government by contracting to put land into
permanent grass cover or trees. This is termed the "conservation reserve" feature of the law. Contracts are for from three
to ten years for grass cover and for up to fifteen years for
trees. The farmer agrees not to pasture the land or take any
kind of a crop from it during the life of the contract. The
"rental" payments will be modest, probably averaging about
ten dollars an acre. This is intended to remove poor land
from production. It ought to be especially attractive to farmers in the "dust bowl" areas of the Great Plains where so
much land was plowed up for wheat during the Second
World War.

In addition to the rental payments, farmers will be able
to get cost-sharing grants for initial practices or structures
needed to convert the land to grass or trees.

Another part of the "soil bank" program is termed the
"acreage reserve." This is designed to induce farmers to
reduce acreage of basic crops below the allotments. For
example, a man who has a corn allotment of 60 acres could
earn payments by reducing his corn acreage by 15 per cent

(down to 51 acres), or more. Payments for this would be much higher than for the conservation reserve and would average about half the gross income expected from normal yields and the guaranteed support price. In the case of good Iowa corn land, this would be about fifty dollars an acre at the 1956 support price. The acreage reserve is expected to be of relatively short duration, and contracts will be for one year at a time. Once the surpluses of corn, wheat, cotton, rice, tobacco, and peanuts are lowered to reasonable levels, presumably this part of the soil bank will be ended.

In effect, the acreage reserve is simply a way of reducing the allotments of basic crops still lower and giving farmers a direct subsidy to hoist their incomes. It is essentially the same as the original (1934) agricultural adjustment program, which provided what were then called "benefit payments" to farmers who complied with the acreage allotments. If history repeats itself, which it probably will, the reduction in output from this cut in basic crop acreage will be short-lived. The march of improved technology is still going on. Farmers probably will soon be able to offset the cut in acreage by stepping up yields, through more fertilizer, irrigation, and improved methods generally. Nevertheless, this may prove to be a good emergency measure.

The agricultural conservation payments program has been working against the acreage allotment program. It has tended to increase output. To be consistent with the national objectives in agricultural adjustment, the payments for output-increasing practices should be eliminated. Subsidies should be paid only for erosion control—not for irrigation, drainage, or the use of fertilizer. The government might as logically give farmers a subsidy for using the new hormone, stilbestrol, in cattle feed as provide financial aid for irrigation.

This applies not only to individual farm practices, but also to public reclamation projects. It is true that comparatively little land is involved in the land reclamation programs. Still, it is foolish to be bringing new farm land into production at the very time when another branch of government is seeking to take land out of use. It is true that in multiple-purpose dam projects the additional cost of opening new land for irrigation is small. But even a small public expenditure for this purpose cannot easily be justified at a time of farm surpluses.

Despite inconsistencies and conflicts in our national land use and development policies, in general one must say these policies since 1935 have been in the broad national interest. Progress has been made toward more efficient use of the soil resource. Erosion has been slowed. Education in better soil husbandry has been effective. The Soil Conservation Service has proved itself as a useful national agency.

Yet, from the viewpoint of agriculture, most of the "conservation" work has intensified the problem of excess supply in relation to demand, just as improved technology in general has.

An unsolved problem is to find ways of reducing the pressure toward greater output. In this, genuine conservation—holding land out of full use—has a part to play.

16

What Is Ahead for Farmers?

"What is a farmer going to do in the next ten years to make a decent living for his family? I'm wondering whether I ought to sell out and do something else."

A farmer friend of mine was speaking. We were watching the stars on a warm July evening from lawn chairs in my back yard. As usual in Iowa in July the topic of conversation had been the weather. We had been moaning about the drought (at that time the Des Moines area was 15 inches short of normal rainfall for the preceding 12 months; normal is about 32 inches) when, out of a clear sky, literally, came the above remark. It was not a question, really, but a comment, made more to himself than to me.

I knew his pessimistic tone was not related to the drought. Jim Adams (as I shall call him here) had just been joshing my wife and me for worrying about the lack of moisture. He had said, "When I started farming I decided not to worry about anything beyond my control—so I never get bothered about the weather. Your lawn will come back. You may lose a shrub or two, but there's no use sweating about it now." Jim was thinking about the long-run prospect for farm profits; he was worrying about the position of farming in the United States economy.

He is a highly successful farmer by anybody's standards. In the eleven years since he came back from the Army, he has greatly improved the 500-acre home farm, the operation of which he took over from his father in 1946. In addition, he has been farming another 300 acres of rented land. He has built up a sizable hog business, feeds a few cattle, and sells a large volume of corn, soybeans, and wheat. His farm is all tillable, flat, productive soil. His buildings are excellent—including an attractive house, modern in all ways. Jim is the epitome of the well-to-do, progressive Iowa farmer.

I must have looked my surprise, for he followed his musing question with, "Oh, I probably won't leave. We like the farm; we like to live in the country; we like the associations of our small community; and we're getting along all right. But I sometimes wonder—I wonder if it's fair to the kids. Their school isn't very good, not compared with your Des Moines schools, for example. But it wasn't that I was thinking about so much as what's ahead for agriculture."

"I never considered you a pessimist, Jim," I said.

"I'm not, really. But I think farming is in for a tough period, about like my father went through in the twenties—not as bad as in the depression, but pretty rough. Our prices are not going to be favorable. And this drive to increase output, improve efficiency is just working against us. You've got to take up each new idea as it comes out—spraying for weeds, new antibiotics in livestock feed, new seed varieties. Right now I'm considering putting in some new wells and trying irrigation. It'll cost a lot of dough. . . . I've got to keep ahead. My costs are going up steeply every year. I've got to step up yields."

"But you fellows who lead the parade in adopting the new methods, you profit from them," I put in.

"Yes, but only for a little while," Jim went on. "Soon everybody's using antibiotics, and production goes up and prices down. If we don't have war, I think the profit in farming is going to be slim for the best of us in the next dozen years. Something's wrong when agriculture can't be really profitable without a war."

"Jim, aren't you overstating the problem a bit? Farmers may not make as much money as during the war, but I can't see disaster looming ahead, as long as general business conditions remain healthy. People are moving out of farming at a rapid rate; those who stay in will have bigger farms, a larger slice of the total farm income of the country. And the government never will let agriculture go to pot—we'll have aid of some sort for farmers. . . ."

"Yes, that's true. Maybe I'm overgloomy right now. But it seems to me the government isn't doing the right things. We subsidize wheat, cotton, corn, peanuts, rice, and tobacco. The livestock man gets little or nothing. Our own farm organizations talk about promotion campaigns for meat, dairy products, and self-help. These don't do much good. I'm not against advertising and promotion. They're helpful. But the whole trend of the economy and buying habits are against much larger spending for food. Americans spend additional income for television sets, cars, and vacations. They eat about as well as they want to eat now. More food available just means lower prices."

"Perhaps ten years of peace will bring more international trade and larger exports of farm products," I said. "I admit I can't see much hope, with all the rest of the world increasing production of food, too. The developing countries of Asia, South America, and Africa can get industrial equipment only by exporting more in the way of basic agricultural products. So the competition in world markets will be rugged. Still, we may be able to sell more abroad if the general world trading situation improves."

"Not enough more to help much. Unless all our high tariff industries, including a good many farm groups, suddenly change their attitudes and agree to a more liberal import policy. I don't see any indication of this. Of course, we can get rid of some farm surpluses by giving them away—but even that seems to be pretty hard to do. Our allies who export farm products resent our giving stuff away, and even the countries who could use more food seem to object to it: their farmers don't want free wheat or rice competing with their products."

Jim Adams is not an "average" farmer, if there is such a thing. He is a college graduate and unusually well informed. He is a former United States Department of Agriculture employee. What he expresses in sophisticated terms, however, is characteristic of what many farmers are thinking at midcentury.

As Jim said to me on another occasion, farmers feel somewhat "left out" in the great prosperity of the 1950's. They feel that the trends of economic growth and development are against them. Many of them have reluctantly come to the conclusion that government programs to protect farm prices, provide subsidies, or otherwise help farmers are here to stay. As recently as in 1948, it seemed to lots of farmers, in Iowa at least, that government programs were on the way out. Farmers were confident that they could get along without government help. All the major farm organizations at that time were in favor of moderate price support levels. But in 1956 it is no longer possible to think of government farm programs as emergency, stopgap devices to help farming over a rough spot. The outlook is for more, not less, government activity in agriculture in the years ahead.

Jim Adams may be ahead of the majority of Iowa farmers in his thinking. He sees the necessity of a change in emphasis in federal farm programs, from basic crop supports to subsidies on livestock and livestock products. Farmer dissatisfaction generally reflects itself still in a demand for higher price guarantees on corn and other basic crops.

Yet it is significant that the National Farmers Organization, which sprang up in Iowa, Missouri, and adjoining states in 1955, pitched its appeal on a demand for twenty-dollar hogs and thirty-dollar cattle. This was the first time that a farm protest group put its major emphasis on livestock. Back in the twenties and thirties the farm leaders, the economists, and the farmers thought that if basic crop prices were supported, this would indirectly benefit livestock producers. The experience of the programs in the thirties and again in the 1948-55 period shows that this does not work out very well.

It is probable that the demand for direct action to protect livestock producers will increase in the years ahead. The National Farmers Organization faded somewhat in 1956 as hog prices began to recover from the low levels of the winter of 1955-56. But it attracted enough members to open the eyes of the established farm organizations. The Farm Bureau in recent years has been expressing increasing concern with the effects of the acreage control and price support programs on livestock farmers. When farmers in the South and Great Plains shift out of cotton and wheat they inevitably turn to feed grains and livestock, and high price support for corn tends to increase the use of other feeds. Altogether, the farm programs gradually swell the output of the livestock industries and exert a downward pressure on prices.

I asked Jim Adams what he proposed to do about the grim outlook he foresaw. He laughed. "Why, I told you. I could sell out and go back to working for the government, or in a bank, or maybe teaching. Seriously, we will cut down—make the old car last longer, do without a vacation trip, postpone remodeling the kitchen. But you mean what do I recommend as a general policy. That isn't so easy. And that's one reason I am a bit pessimistic.

"Frankly, I dislike the idea of trying to guarantee livestock prices. The problems of surpluses in grain are nothing to what they would be if the government started buying pork and beef to support prices. That's out."

"What about outright subsidies to farmers?" I asked.

"I don't like that, either. At least not subsidies on livestock. I suppose you could have subsidies like those we had during the war—with the packers adding a certain amount onto the farmer's sale check and being reimbursed by the government. I think that might work out all right from an administrative standpoint. It would avoid the difficulties of government storage and disposal of meat. But it would certainly increase the incentives to expand production. That would mean lower market prices, larger subsidies. Ultimately, it would mean quotas on livestock. I don't like that idea. Still, we may have to come to it as the only way of protecting the livestock producer."

"What about marketing agreements among farmers? I mean like the milk marketing agreements and the agreements among some fruit and vegetable growers to divert low-quality stuff away from the market and to stabilize marketings and prices."

"Marketing agreements may be a possibility," Jim replied. "But there are so many hog producers all over the country. It's comparatively easy to get a few hundred dairymen around a large city and a few distributors to agree on milk prices and a diversion program. But think of the problems of trying to do that on a national scale with 2 million or more hog producers!"

"It seems to me that you are saying livestock farmers are in trouble because of production's increasing faster than demand, but you don't see any way out."

"Not quite right," said Jim. "I don't see any *easy* or wholly palatable way out. But I do see some things that could be done to improve the situation. I think we should try some method of stabilizing livestock producers' returns. We won't know what can be done until we try. Also, we ought to make it easy for people to get into and out of agriculture. It's the difficulty in getting out of farming into something else that keeps farm income low. If more people moved out faster when incomes are dropping, that would help both those who move out and those who stay."

Jim Adams will not quit farming. And his family will not suffer because of it. His youngsters will go to college; they will have every opportunity. But the fact that a successful farmer like Jim even thinks about leaving the farm is a clue to the mood of farmers created by the decline in income since 1951.

The "farm problem," which really is a whole group of problems, as I have tried to explain in this book, will be with us for a long time to come. In some ways we are making progress. The farm organizations, the Department of Agriculture, and the important leaders on farm affairs in Congress now are all aware of the importance of the poverty sector of agriculture. A start is being made toward bringing technical assistance through the state Extension Services to the poorest farmers in the country. Fifty counties have been selected for intensive experimental programs in helping low-income farm families to improve their status. Agricultural economists and rural sociologists have been talking about the stagnation of farming in certain areas, especially the South, for twenty-five years or more. Now there are a few signs that positive action may be taken. At least the politically important groups are now alerted to the problem.

But so far few steps are being taken to increase the mobility of people out of agriculture. The federal-state employment services do very little to help young farm people to get city jobs. Education in farm areas still is geared heavily to agriculture and does not prepare young people adequately for city work and life.

So far as agricultural production adjustment, price stabilization, and income stabilization for commercial agriculture are concerned, progress has been slight. It is true that we know a great deal about stabilizing supplies and prices of basic crops, as a result of twenty-three years' experience, but the lessons have not been followed in practice. As for the more difficult problems of stabilizing vegetable, fruit, livestock, and livestock product prices, the record is not encouraging.

In a democracy social invention has to proceed slowly. Quick panaceas are viewed with suspicion, and rightly so.

Americans want farming to be a healthy industry and a satisfactory way of life. They want farmers to be paid by society in proportion to their contribution to society, as urban workers are. The same amount of skill and productivity ought to command the same income whether in farming or in steel making. But Americans do not want to adopt rigid government controls aimed at achieving this equality if these should mean sacrificing the initiative, the independence, and the freedom of the farm family.

The continued health of a primarily family type agriculture is important to America. A "solution" to the farm income problem which resulted in a factory type farm system would not appeal to many people, farm or nonfarm. On the other hand, a "solution" which froze farming into its present organizational pattern and prevented further progress in farm efficiency would not be in the national interest.

So we will continue to muddle along by compromise, experimentation, and half-measures. This is the way of democracy, and it is the best way.

Index